Thank you for reading! Mari

Jacksonville

*One Mom's Journey To The Autism
Spectrum*

Jacksonville

One Mom's Journey To The Autism Spectrum

by

Mari Sandifer

Pipe Dream Publishing

Copyright

Pipe Dream Publishing
5250 Tammany Trail
Carmel, IN 46033

Copywrite Registration Number: TXu 2-155-171

Hardback ISDN: 978-1-7342216-0-2
Paperback ISDN: 978-1-7342216-1-9
marisandiferbooks.com
marisandifer.com

Dedication

For Ed, Betsy and Jack.

I sought the Lord and He answered me and delivered me from all my fears.

Psalm 34:4

Mari Sandifer

Table of Contents

Acknowledgements

Ed, being married to me is not for the faint of heart. Thank you for never giving up on me. The vastness of those who call you friend speaks to your loyalty and vibrant personality. Wherever you are, there too, is the gift of laughter. Thank you for pushing Jack even when I objected. Especially when I objected. He would not be where he is today without you. Nor would I. Nor would any of us.

Betsy, you are an old soul and the love you have shown your brother throughout the years brings me to my knees. You were Jack's live-in speech therapist and the embodiment of joy in our home. There is a light you bring to every situation that is uniquely your own and I am proud to call you my daughter. Continue to follow your dreams. They know the way.

Hilton Head Island, 2007.

Mari Sandifer

Jack, this book is for and about you. You are the most tender-hearted, genuinely kind person I know. When you read the chapters of this book about the early years when I was sad that you had autism, when you had tantrums, pulled my hair, and headbutted me, you will want to apologize a million times. You will feel bad for something over which you had no control. I want to take this opportunity to apologize a million times to you--for *ever* wishing that you were different than you are. You are without guile. Fully joyful. My greatest gift. Thank you for making me softer. Thank you for enriching my life with your unique perspective. Thank you for your unconditional love and the joy you have brought me as we have gone on adventures together. As you pass me up in height and your voice deepens, I'm in awe of the man you are becoming. But at the same time, I recall the golden-haired boy with clear, cornflower blue eyes who captured my heart and changed me. The boy who taught me to notice. To see.

Walter Bode, you were not only my editor, but my long-distance therapist. This book simply would not exist without you. Thank you, Curtis Honeycutt, for meeting with me on several occasions to discuss this project, to encourage one another in our writing, and to compare anti-depressant medications. Thank you, Amy Snow, for being my life coach and friend over the years. You see me fully, yet you never look away. Thank you, Amy Christie, for telling me I should write my story after I presented my "life in a bag" at our Grace Church drama group meeting in 2014. You watered a seed that I didn't even know was there.

Thank you, Debbie Lynn, for speaking life into this

project in 2015 when you visited from California, and for connecting me with my editor, Walt. Thank you, Vicki Burdick, for your friendship of forty-plus years. You come from a place of "Yes, and…" That is your superpower. I love you.

Debbie, Me, and Vicki 1985.

Thank you to my brother, Drew Hammond, for creating the pipe organ logo that perfectly captures the essence of The Jacksonville Foundation and Pipe Dream Publishing. To my Nephew, Ben Meador, thank you for the beautiful music you composed and performed that will be used during the taping of the audio version of this book. You are a gift to our family. Thank you to my cousin, Steve Appel. Always the cheerleader. Always forthcoming with input and encouragement. Always smiling. God bless you, Renee Alberts & Diane Knollman. You were Jack's first teachers and remain friends to this day. Keep doing what you are doing. You are making a difference in the world.

Thank you to my beta readers who gave so generously of their time reading this when it was a hot mess: Renee Alberts, Beth Bates, Vicki Burdick, Jenni Hammond, John Hammond, Diane Knollman, Debbie Lynn, Missy Meador, Sue Rosecrans, Ed Sandifer, Betsy Sandifer, Jack Sandifer, John Stewart, and Mary Kaye Wells.

Thank you to my parents, John and Norma Hammond, and Jim and Kay Sandifer. Thank you for providing support and wisdom over the years. Thank you for coming alongside us on our journey and for teaching us to love the Lord.

May this book glorify His name.

Dear Beta Reader,

Thank you so much for helping my mother on this special project. My mom has been working on this book for over a year and taking many time slots to write chapters of the book, summarizing important moments of my life, and background of my mother. This can bring special awareness to parents of those who are on the spectrum. I'm hoping that this book will solve many problems of the mothers and fathers that are concerned of their kids. I know my mother was very worried about me when I was just a toddler. Thankfully, special teachers and friends of my mom helped her see the light at the end of the tunnel. Again, thank you ever so much for being helpful to my mother. I highly appreciate it.

Sincerely,
Jack Sandifer

Mari Sandifer

Foreword

Through humor and heartbreaking honesty, Jacksonville is an account of a mother's personal journey navigating parenthood with a child with developmental challenges leading to a diagnosis of autism spectrum disorder. It was an unexpected trial in Mari's vision for the perfect life for her and her family.

The detour on life's road began with inklings of differences in her son's development. Then there was the question, "Do you think Jack has autism, Diane?" And then the gentle, honest answer from me, "Yes, I do." I knew that Mari's new emotional obstacle was a mere detour, because her love for her son was big enough and deep enough to conquer all the confusion, denial, and grief that hit her with my simple "yes." There was no doubt that Mari had a heart brimming over with love for her little man.

I have been blessed, since the age of 14, to have walked beside individuals with exceptional needs and to have learned from them all the best life has to offer! I have been enlightened and educated by the finest individuals in the world and have experienced the life lessons of unconditional love, compassion, faith, trust, humility, and understanding. To realize the significance of life from a person that the world often overlooks or even disregards is like sharing in a divine secret. I have had the privilege of journeying with babies, children, adolescents, and adults with disabilities, as well as with their families.

Blessed beyond measure! My first marriage proposal

came from a young adult with Down syndrome named Kenny who, shortly after that proposal, died from heart defects he had had since birth. I will never forget the sincerity of his love, and his acceptance of the fact that I couldn't even cook. He agreed to a life of peanut butter and jelly! So many stories and so much joy and love received! My heart has been etched with the innumerable names and faces and has grown exponentially bigger. One such family, carved on the bark of my heart is the Sandifer family, especially Jack!

If you have chosen this book chances are *you* have a story that belongs to you alone. I have been blessed to walk the road to acceptance with many, many parents in my career as an educator of children and adults with special needs, and their journeys are all unique. I myself have traveled my own personal path, though I admit my walk began much differently than Mari's. Because I began as an instructor for adults with Developmental Disabilities, I had a very good look at the future, the possibilities, the opportunities, and the wonderful "gems" that were once wrapped gifts that were not exactly what their parents expected.

Every child comes as a wrapped gift. At times, the wrapping is a little different or unexpected, but sometimes the wrapping is just perfect, but at the first reveal, you discover your child has autism. Look closer. Once the gem inside is exposed the genuine beauty shines forth. Your child has a unique personality, extraordinary gifts and unconditional love.

When I heard the gentle whisper from our Heavenly Father, to adopt a child with Down syndrome, of course I had some fear. What would the future look like? A very wise mother, who coordinated adoptions with the Cincinnati Down Syndrome Association answered that question with another question, "Do you know the future of ANY of your biological children?"

Mari's story of her passage to acceptance is unique to her, and she has courageously shared it with transparent honesty. As readers you may see yourself in her unfiltered grief, fear, shame, loss of control, confusion, doubt, and, yes, surrender and acceptance.

This story must be told, because Mari is one of many mothers who struggle when a plan unexpectedly unravels. Her story must be told because that was part of her "God assigned instructions" sent with her son. Her purpose was revealed as she watched Jack grow and as she experienced the great gifts within him. No, our kids don't come with a handbook, but God desires to share the gifts of individuals with the world in unique ways.

Jacksonville speaks volumes about Mari's fears and grief for her son, but also to the awesome revelation of what Jack brings to our world!! God sends surprises, our children with autism, to remind us that all lives have a purpose. From these gems we learn the life lessons of unconditional love, trust, simplicity, compassion, true happiness, acceptance, and genuine joy!

Diane Knollman,

Jack's preschool teacher

Betsy, Jack, me, and Diane, 2019.

Preface

Flat vocal patterns. Lack of eye contact. Anxiety over any small change in routine. A child who spends recess walking in circles, waxing poetic about engine coolant. A teenager who has difficulty with basic reciprocal conversation skills but has an uncanny ability to memorize train schedules or narrate all the *Zoolander* movies. In 1994, the American Psychiatric Association (APA) decided that this kind of diverse array of symptoms added up to a diagnosis called Asperger's Disorder (also known as Asperger's Syndrome) and added it to the 4th edition of the *Diagnostic and Statistical Manual of Mental Disorders* (DSM). Asperger's quickly became synonymous with a kind of high-functioning autism in which children struggled with social skills, anxiety, and repetitive or restrictive behaviors, but also tended to display impressive cognitive and verbal abilities. In 2013, the diagnosis of Asperger's was removed from the Diagnostic and Statistical Manual of Mental Disorders (DSM-5), and people with these symptoms are now included within the autism spectrum disorder along with autism and pervasive developmental disorder not otherwise specified (PDD-NOS). I am going to continue to use the term Asperger's throughout the book as I believe it helps in identifying where people like Jack fall on the autism spectrum, which is vast indeed.

Our son, Jack, has high functioning autism. On the other end of the spectrum are children who are non-verbal and virtually unable to connect. This book is not about them. If you have a child on that end of the autism spectrum my prayers are with you and my story will sound superficial. But it's my journey, and if it speaks to anyone, I'm glad to tell it. I've been writing this book in my head for over 14 years. When I took the picture on the cover in 2013, I knew it would be used for this book, and that the name of the book would be "Jacksonville". Jack has a beautiful imagination. When he was little and became enchanted with the story in his head, he would gallop around the house humming with a terrific smile on his face. My husband and I would joke and say things like, "They must have inflated the bounce houses in Jacksonville" or "The ice cream truck must be in Jacksonville." I never thought Jack noticed until one day when I asked, "Jack, what are you pretending? I want to go there. It sounds delightful!" He looked at me and said, "I've gone to Jacksonville, and you're not invited."

I don't write too much about Betsy or Ed in this book, not because they weren't there or intimately involved, but because I respect their privacy. If they want to tell this story from their points of view, they will someday. Most of the recollections in this book are of the struggles that went on in my head. For each person this was a solitary journey.

Jack age 9, Thanksgiving Day, 2011.

Autism … offers a chance for us to glimpse an awe-filled vision of the world that might otherwise pass us by.

Dr. Colin Zimbleman, Phd

Mari Sandifer

Chapter 1 -Yes

It is Fall, 2005. Jack is three years old. I am looking out my bedroom window while talking on the phone with Jack's preschool teacher, Diane Knollman. It's overcast outside. The neighborhood pool is empty and closed for the season, except for an abandoned beach ball lying on the deck. Its bright colors mock my inner turmoil. I hate that ball.

> Me: Do you think he has autism?
> Diane: Yes.
> Silence.
> Diane: I'm sorry.
> Me (on autopilot): It's okay.
> Diane: No. It's not.

On that grey day Diane answered swiftly and with clarity because she knew where I was on my journey. She knew that at that moment *it was not OK*. Diane has a son with Down syndrome. She could have encouraged me with stories of how frightened she had been in the beginning and how far her son, Patrick, has come. But there are times, I have learned, when the most comforting thing one can bring to another person's heartbreak is a compassionate silence. I can assure you that I wouldn't have remembered anything Diane would have said. But I do recall with crystal clarity how she made me feel: supported, loved, understood, and most importantly: not a bad mother. Not a bad mother. Not a bad mother. That reassurance was balm to my soul.

If you were guaranteed an honest response to one question, whom would you ask and what would you ask of them?

Maya Angelou

Chapter 2 – It's Good to Be Mari

Mari, Betsy, Ed and Jack (in-utero), 2001.

Oh, to be young and in control. And ridiculously naïve. Life was good in The Land of Mari back in the summer of 2001. Here's what success meant to my 34-year-old brain: you go to college, get a job, marry someone, have a couple of kids, and buy a four-bedroom house. I was well on my way to checking all the boxes. My husband Ed and I had a sweet little two-year-old girl named Betsy, and the cable had just been hooked up at our new house. I had my full-time job at Ernst & Young, and Ed's mom (a retired second grade teacher) was providing free childcare. Forty-eight hours after we moved in, I took a pregnancy test and it was positive. I wasn't surprised because having a second child was on my Excel spreadsheet for 2002, and when you combine being a control freak with dogged determination and lots of hard work, things tend to go as planned. The problem with that is two-fold:

1. You think all of life's good fortune is a direct result of your efforts.

2. You are woefully ill-equipped when the shit hits the fan. And the shit *always* hits the fan.

The week of April 7, 2002 went as planned, because everything basically did back then. I cleaned the house, colored my hair, did my nails, and dropped Betsy off at Ed's parents' house. On Wednesday, April 10, 2002, we said a prayer in the car and drove over to St. Vincent Hospital for my scheduled C-Section. It was a heady time. So many plans and dreams.

There is a time in early adulthood when if you have done the prudent things, if you have delayed gratification and been wise, you start to see the fruits. It is glorious. Because you have pride in the fact that you are "doing life well." There is the expectation that you will continue to make wise choices and reap the benefits of clean living. That was the season I was in, and the air was crisp and fragrant. Humidity was low and the temperature was a perpetual 72 degrees. I was young and proud of the family we were creating. Of course, the sun would continue to shine. Of course, I would continue to do all the right things…

Because Betsy had been born via cesarean section, I had the option to have this procedure for any subsequent births. Having this choice is a control freak's dream! I had never defined my womanhood by the ability to push something the size of a small watermelon through my lady parts, and I had found the painkillers given to me after Betsy's c-section to be quite delightful. Also, I could decide (within a week or so) when I would deliver. We hadn't chosen to know our baby's gender in advance, but for some reason I assumed it would be another girl. Imagine my surprise when Dr. Timothy Feeney announced, "He has a penis."

But it didn't take me long to accept this miracle as my due. Another box checked. Another score for our side. We were only going to have two children (and someone like me never gets pregnant by accident), so one of each kind seemed perfect. Ed and I used to say, "Cue the deer" * in situations where things were just too good to be true.

April 10, 2002.

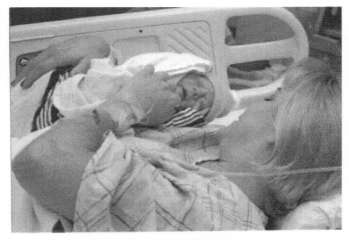

April 10, 2002.

* The expression "cue the deer" comes from *Funny Farm,* in a scene where a couple are showing their home to prospective buyers. The sellers want to make their home as attractive as possible. As the potential buyers approach the home, <u>Chevy Chase's</u> characters says "cue the deer" into a <u>walkie-talkie</u> and a small deer is released from a cage and scampers across the lawn, charming the socks right off the buyers.

As parents, Ed and I had been blessed with a first child who was a regular show pony. Betsy's speech and developmental progress were off the charts. She sang show tunes and "God Bless America" on cue (this was post-9/11, so her rendition often elicited tears), she recited the Christmas story verbatim as told by the Gospel of Luke and pretended to read books she had memorized.

I recall sitting with her on the floor at my sister Missy's house with some friends. Betsy's request for more Steak and Shake "hexagon crackers" brought eye-rolls from my sister and her friend Cathy McQuiston, who asked, "So when are you going to have another one, Mari? Jump into the pit with the rest of us." I recall feeling smug, and sure that any subsequent child would be just like Betsy.

Betsy aged 9 months, 2000.

The only pit involved would be the pit of balls at Chuck E. Cheese, where we would make priceless family memories together. The good thing about Betsy's charm and precociousness was that it was easy for Ed and me to draw an unbroken line between our good decisions and our perfect life. The bad thing about Betsy's charm and precociousness was that it was easy for Ed and me to draw an unbroken line between our good decisions and our perfect life. I was ready to assume that line would extend to our new baby boy.

There is this very nice anti-nausea medication they give to those of us who are prone to barfing post-epidural. No one wants to retch into the kidney shaped bowl after having had their abdominal muscles hacked through, and the medication makes one extremely sleepy. I welcomed that because I had not slept a wink the night before. What made that "sink-into-the-mattress, mommy go night-night" feeling even more glorious was that I could drift off while mentally ticking off the items on my list of everything about my life that was ideal. I distinctly remember lying on my left side thinking how absolutely perfect my life was. And that somehow, I deserved all of it. Husband. Job. House. Girl. Boy…zzzzz.

These are the things I knew that night:

1. His hair had the glint of sunshine's kiss.

2. He was beautiful.

3. Our family was complete.

4. Life was sweet—just as I had always envisioned it would be.

Let us not pray to be sheltered from dangers but to be fearless when facing them.

Rabindranath Tagore, 1916

Chapter 3 – Who's a Good Boy!?

J ack was an easy baby, especially compared to Betsy, who kept us on the run. To this day, if I text "0015" or write it anywhere, Ed will know what it means. We attend a megachurch, the kind that is so big it has multiple digital signs that flash numbers to let you know that your child needs to be picked up from the nursery. Those red lights were the bat phone for any skittish mother, which I was. They could mean anything from "Johnny just blew out his diaper and needs new pants" to "Johnny just choked on a Skittle but we Heimliched him so it's okay." And it's nothing to scoff at. Those nursery workers are a scrappy lot. They take their responsibility to keep a child for seventy-five minutes so that stressed out parents can worship Jesus very seriously. I have volunteered in the nursery countless times, and I am continually humbled by the herculean efforts these people make to avoid having to summon a parent.

Without fail, for the first three years of Betsy's life, our number came up. 0015. Within fifteen minutes. Every Sunday. That was Betsy's number. You see, Betsy, too, is hard-core. And whip smart. She had an array of tools she could draw upon to get mom and/or dad back. There were the traditional tools that all children seem to know instinctively: crying, hyperventilating, screaming, pleading with whatever words are at their command. Pushed to the limit, most have the option of wetting their pants. But Betsy had a secret weapon that was supremely effective: projectile vomiting.

Ding! Ding! Ding! Get that girl a parent!

She found a formula that worked. And she used it. Every week. Outside of church, Betsy *really* liked to be carried. She also liked being jostled a bit, like in those bouncy, vibrating chairs. Except that it couldn't be a chair. It had to be Ed or me. When carried, she demanded that we walked or stood. Sitting (or leaning, for that matter) was not acceptable. If she sensed that we were not fully engaging every muscle of our body in the act of holding her, there was hell to pay. A new mother, I was scared to death to be responsible for this baby and terribly concerned with how I appeared to be faring as a mom, so I did *whatever* it took to keep her quiet. The words most often said to me at a party or a get-together were: "Mari, sit down." The words I said in return were always, "Oh, no I can't." I meant, *"Really. I can't."*

Wishing I could sit down, 2000.

Mari Sandifer

Jack, on the other hand, was a breath of fresh air. I was astonished that it was possible to have a baby that I could pass off to anyone. A baby I could lay down anywhere with no tears, screams, or release of bodily fluids. We called Jack our "potted plant" because basically all we had to do was feed him and watch him grow.

The first twelve months of his life were textbook. He was not sick at all. No ear infections. Slept through the night at three months, sat up on time, walked at twelve months, smiled, engaged, clapped, ate well, and adored being snuggled. I had learned my lesson with Betsy that the baby years went fast. I also knew this was my last child, so I took every opportunity to hold this little man. Every night I swaddled him tightly and held him for at least an hour. His sister adored him from the start and could make him laugh like no one else. He was completely different from her as a baby, yet they bonded and were drawn to each other from the start in a way that was miraculous to watch. We have a video of Ed flying Jack into Betsy's tummy to make her laugh. At six days old, he was playing with his sister and making her laugh down to her toes. That has never stopped. Watching the two of them together has been one of the greatest gifts of my life. I often forget that they came from me because their relationship is so unusual that I imagine them as angels sent to teach Ed and me lessons. But I didn't know any of this back then. I still thought that everything was coming up roses because I was doing all the right things. When I watch home videos from this time, I actually feel sorry for my thirty-four-year-old self. She still thinks she is in control.

Betsy, age 3; Jack, 5 months.

My husband and I have a tradition of writing a letter to our children every year on their birthday. While writing this book I read through Jack's to help spark memories. It was a bit haunting to read our notes with hindsight, but it helped me recall his development, which was right on track as a baby. As mentioned earlier, autism often presents itself as a "lack of affect." A flat response. As a baby, Jack was as animated as any other child, although less than Betsy had been. In his first birthday letter I noted that he liked to lie on his back and hold his own bottle, but that I often snuck him into my arms to hold him. I enjoyed that so, because Betsy had never like that. We used to lay him on the couch in the family room before he could roll over, and he would burrow his little head against a pillow to fall asleep. He used to fight the sleep and would be still and then thrash about before eventually succumbing. It was funny to watch. We thought he looked like a bug that had just been sprayed.

One thing that made him furious, when he became old enough to get around independently, was getting dressed. He couldn't stand to be held in placed or restrained in any manner. Sounds of his anguish could be heard throughout the house as his dad or I tried to clothe him. He loved to play with toys and watch Baby Einstein videos. When we used to come to get him, he had a way of showing his glee by kicking his legs (if someone was holding him), grinning and throwing his head back. It was quite a welcome.

He was not walking consistently on his first birthday but was taking three or four steps at a time. He loved Cheerios and crackers, having a ball bounced to him, watching Dad and Betsy play, being carried, taking a bath, being outside, Grandma and Grandpa's cat Lucy, going in the laundry room and shrieking, pulling toilet paper off the roll, going into the basement, pulling hair and necklaces, crawling to Daddy when he got home, being thrown in the air, swinging outside and any type of cord. He was spot on in hitting his developmental milestones. When we used to lay him down in the bathtub on his yellow foam pad, Betsy and I would pour warm water over his flawless little body and he would put his hands behind his head like a man resting in a hammock as if to say, "My women. They wash me."

Those were such simple, precious days. Whenever he saw me, he immediately crawled over and pulled up on my leg. His only desire was for me to pick him up and hold him. I knew these times were fleeting so I relished every moment. I was so sure I was doing everything just right. Looking back, I now realize that being completely sure of anything is never a good place to be.

Mari and Jack, May 2002.

He reached for me and I held him tight, the boy with fair hair and ocean blue eyes. The one that made me feel so alive.

Christy Ann Martone

Chapter 4 – Houston, We Have a Problem

J ack's time as an infant was textbook. It wasn't until he was about eighteen months that I started watching him more closely. And watching other toddlers more closely to compare. I can't recall a specific event that made me wonder if something was not right with his development. It was more like that time when I was shopping at the Fashion Mall and had a weird feeling as I left a particular store. Something felt off. When I got to my car, I realized that my keys were missing. I recalled the odd feeling I had upon leaving Talbots and sure enough, I found them there, lying next to a stack of cotton turtlenecks. It was a sixth sense kind of thing. That's how this felt.

The early 2000's was a heavily regimented time filled with schedules and lists. Saturday mornings were for the grocery with Betsy and Jack. I marvel now at my dogmatic dedication to rising early, showering, doing my make-up and hair, dressing the kids and getting to Marsh Supermarket by ten so that we could get to my grandmother's by eleven for our weekly visit. I was also hypervigilant about the cleanliness of the house and the strict "chore schedule" that I adhered to. Cleaning the house once a week, laundry on Wednesdays and Saturdays, dry Swiffering on Tuesdays and Thursdays etc... I routinely strapped the kids into their car seats only to dash back into the house for 30 seconds to throw all misplaced toys into a basket. It made perfect sense. What if we all died in a car accident? What would the police/chaplain think when they came to tell Ed and there were Polly Pocket dresses all over the floor? They would think me a bottom feeding hobo mother. That's what they would think.

My parents, John and Norma Hammond, lived across the street from my grandmother, Eloise, and they would join us on these Saturday visits. Jack was not talking as much as Betsy had, but we attributed that to him being a different person with a different personality. When I look back on these times my mind is filled with a barrage of memories. Traditions we enjoyed: The Keebler cookie display at Marsh that we visited every Saturday as we shopped, a mechanical horse that Betsy rode, and then Jack - when he was old enough, my dad hoisting Betsy to Eloise's grandfather clock and jabbing her ribs playfully as the hours chimed, him pretending to chase our car as we left while the kids laughed. My Grandma Eloise plying Betsy with cookies and bringing out her stash of 5-7 toys made special because they were only to be found at her house. One Saturday they were having a neighborhood garage sale. What fun we had going from garage to garage with Jack in the stroller and Betsy searching for treasures.

Jack with Grandma Norma, 2002.

Betsy with Grandpa John, 2002.

Jack's Grandma Norma and Great-Grandma Eloise, 2003.

Eventually, gymnastics and dance lessons for Betsy replaced these visits, my grandmother passed, and her house was sold. I wish I had known that the last time I pretended to try and "out drive my running father" was the last time I would ever do that, but such is life. The days dragged and the years flew. I worked full time and was determined to balance motherhood, work, and keeping the house. I truly don't know how I did it in retrospect. I look back on it now with wonder and at times ask myself if it was all just a dream.

However, in all the "busyness" I did realize and feel that something was wrong with Jack. But I was not yet ready to acknowledge this. And I hoped I was wrong. When I review the letter I wrote to him on his second birthday it breaks my heart a bit. Because I know that the letter is leaving my fears out. It puts on a brave face, because when I wrote it, I pictured him reading it later and hoped these fears would be unfounded.

From Jack's 2-year old birthday letter, dated April 10, 2004:

We quickly realized that you are a bit more adventurous than your big sister. Our first clue was when you had minor surgery to open your tear duct at fourteen months. They inserted a very small tube to be removed in a month's time. But you decided to remove the tube yourself the afternoon of the surgery. As we were driving home. We are not sure how you did it, but I was in the car driving on Carmel Drive and I looked back at you only to see something strange lying across the bridge of your nose. It was shiny, like a string of spit. I pulled over and sure enough, you had decided the tube wasn't for you! I called the doctor and he said you won the prize for the speediest "self-removal" he had ever known. Thankfully, your eye healed and no reinsertion was necessary!

We have found you sitting/standing on the tray of your highchair, sitting on end tables, sitting on the bookshelf of the family room, standing on the back of the piano. You are like an "Elf on a Shelf". You have gone headfirst out of your crib and headfirst into Betsy's bath; fully clothed.

Mari Sandifer

Your latest trick was climbing into the dryer. You were so proud and comfortable in there, laying back with elbows resting on the interior ledges as if unwinding in a La-Z Boy recliner!

You are a smart and determined little soul—very focused on whatever interests you. I love watching you "read" books or attempt anything that entails manual dexterity. I believe you have gifts in these areas and look forward to seeing them develop. You love to be read to and often request the same book over and over by shouting, "AGAIN! AGAIN!" You are learning all the time and I love to watch you observe your sister. You study her so intently and smile often as you do—you love her so! And she can't keep her hands off you! She often chases you around the room as you squeal.

Jack's second birthday, April 10, 2004.

During this time Ed's mom, Kay, was watching the kids three days a week while I worked. Being a retired second grade teacher, she relished having Betsy and Jack in their home during this time. Ed's father, Jim, was a semi-retired attorney practicing out of his home office. We couldn't have crafted a better situation for all involved. Practically speaking, my friends were paying a lot of money each month for childcare. We were not. But on a deeper level, my children were being cherished, taught and guided by people we admired and loved. Every time I tried to put my thanks into words I was met with some form of the following: "Our home is filled with such love and joy when they are here. We are thrilled to be able to do this. What else would we possibly do with our time?" What more is there to say? It was a blessing that we will never be able to repay or to adequately acknowledge with words.

Kay kept a journal during this time that records Jack's development, typical for an eighteen to twenty-four-month-old boy.

Notes from Kay dated Monday, January 5, 2004:

Grandpa Jim and Betsy, 2000.

Second try at a journal with a second grandchild. Jack is almost 21 months old and not verbal like Betsy but likes to explore. Cheerios are #1. Jack is very musically oriented. He bounces to the melody on the radio or VHS. Like Betsy, he loves the Baby Einstein series. Animals entertain him. While Betsy likes dolls, Jack likes anything with wheels. Jack loves shapes and tries to say their names. He also enjoys books and listens fairly well. He jabbers and points to the words. Jack has a killer smile and says, "no-no" while touching something he knows he is not supposed to. He is *fast*. One day he grabbed a Haviland plate and went running through the living room.

Grandpa Jim and Grandma Kay with Jack, 2002.

I wish I had kept a personal journal during that time. One that only I would see. I should have had a place to share my concerns openly instead of keeping them all inside and trying to hide them by making our house beautiful and dressing everyone to perfection. No one wants to think there is something wrong with their child but woven throughout the everyday activities I did start to see things that looked off. He didn't respond to my overexaggerated attempts to engage. He seemed to look right through me.

And once I did get his attention, it was difficult to maintain. I kept it to myself at the time but knowing what I know now I can see that these were warning signs.

The large church we attend has not just "a nursery". There is *a wing* of nursery rooms. Each one for a certain age or level of development. When my children were young, they had cute animal names: Puppy Dogs (infants), Monkeys (crawlers), and Jack's nursery: the Frogs (new walkers). Parents would come up to a counter at the front of the room and call out to their child. Then the parent would (a) bask in being treated like Beyoncé when their child ran to them screaming in delight, or (b) grin and bear them breaking down into tears, as in "I forgot you left me but now that I am reminded, I realize all over again how much I love you because you are absolutely the best mom/dad EVER and now I must weep for joy!" When we came for Jack, however, he never looked up from his board book no matter how many people called his name.

Super awkward.

"He must be at the 'quiet old lady whispering hush' part," we joked. It didn't happen only at church. We have a video of Thanksgiving morning 2003, when he was eighteen months, taken as we were leaving for Jim and Kay's house. Jack is watching the Macy's Thanksgiving Day Parade on television, his back to the camera. I call his name. No response. I call "Jack!" several times. Ed calls him too. Nothing. I can then be heard saying something like "He must be riveted by the Sponge Bob float," …but inside I was panicking.

About this time, he started doing an unusual thing with his body when something excited him. He would kind of

Jack not responding to his name after several tries, 18 months.

stand to attention and then prance on his toes in delight, garnering the nickname "twinkle toes." We also noticed that he didn't like looking directly at people. This was evident by the way he seemed to grimace and physically recoil when approached by the ultra-animated who were hoping to make a connection. This works great with typical children, and they love it. Jack, not so much. It was as if he were being made to stare directly into the sun. His workaround was to close one eye, which was almost as adorable as the toe walking. We referred to this as giving someone the "the pirate eye." He would also sometimes hold objects out to the side of his head, squint; and shake what he was holding. We didn't have a name for that, because it wasn't cute. It was weird. We would later come to know that this is called "visual play" and is a marker for autism. The child is enjoying watching the object move in their peripheral vision.

Sometimes he would sit very still and extend his hand

gingerly, as if reaching for something quite specific and exquisitely precious. Was he seeing dust glinting in the sun? Or something that only he could see? It was mysterious, beautiful, and terrifying all at once. Ed and I both noticed these things, hence the funny nicknames we gave some of his behaviors. But we did not discuss with one another that we thought anything was amiss. At the time, Ed just saw Jack as a "cool customer." Some kids, like Betsy, "gave it away for free," but Jack didn't suffer fools. He was nobody's puppet. I liked that and hoped beyond hope that Ed's interpretation was correct.

At the park one day, I looked down at Jack sitting in the grass. I was standing behind him, watching Betsy go down the slide, so I was looking down on him from above. He was holding one blade of grass in each hand horizontally, and with the dexterity of a neurosurgeon, slowly moving them toward each other and tapping the tips together. Tap. Tap. Tap. He never missed - they always touched perfectly.

Neurosurgeon? Maybe. Strange? Definitely.

All these small moments. Separately, nothing. But like tiny droplets on a windshield, they converged and rolled. After eighteen months, it was obvious that he had changed. It seemed like someone had turned the lights off behind his eyes. His countenance had lost its animation and become flat. There was a distance that hadn't been there before. When he looked at me, he seemed to be looking right through me (see exhibit A).

Exhibit A

Jack – 12 months   Jack – 18 months

I remember a specific day from that time. I was returning from work at Ernst & Young and pulling up to Jim and Kay's house on a cul-de-sac to get the kids. I saw Jack standing in the driveway watching the car approach. He was holding a broom in his right hand and a yellow golf club in his left. He had recently taken to carrying stick-shaped items—golf clubs, brooms, umbrellas, etc. I anticipated having to brake suddenly, figuring that once he realized I was driving the car he would charge headlong toward me in delirious glee as he had in the past.

Except that he didn't.

I pulled into the driveway, stopped, and got out of the car. He just stood like a statue and stared at me, or through me. Maybe, I thought, he was pretending, just messing with me. Or maybe he was spacing out, as people sometimes do. No. He was staring right at me, but in a weird way that caused me to look around; to see if anyone else was behind me. Part of me wanted a witness, a second opinion, but most of me didn't. "HI, BABY!" I said, way too loud, way too animated.

Nothing. Holy crap.

I had mentioned in passing to others that I was concerned because Jack wasn't talking. He was using single words here and there—but nothing like other kids his age and certainly nothing like his sister when she was two. Other parents would relieve my worries by saying things like, "boys always speak later," or that I was "just used to Betsy and her high-school vocabulary," or that "Einstein didn't talk until he was five."

I started a similar conversation with Jennifer Jansen in the spring of 2004 when Jack was two. Jennifer is one of my best friends. We met in the eighth grade, went to Indiana University together, and are sorority sisters.

Jennifer graduated Phi Beta Kappa with a BA in Psychology and holds a master's degree in social work. She introduced me to my husband. She is virtually incapable of blowing smoke. She is a genuine and lifelong friend. I asked her about Jack one day. I expected, what I secretly hoped, was that she'd repeat those bland and comforting reassurances.

She didn't.

"I do see some things in how he interacts with others that concern me," she confided with care in her voice. "You should have him tested by First Steps. They are an early intervention program that provides services to infants and toddlers who have developmental delays. They'll send a speech therapist right to your house, and it's free if he qualifies."

Bitch.

How dare she??

When I complained to Ed about it later, he aptly asked if I would have preferred for her to lie to me? And pointed out that it had been I who had broached the subject, not Jen.

Jen and me at the Kappa Alpha Theta House, 1988.

"Don't walk in front of me; I may not follow. Don't walk behind me; I may not lead. Just walk beside me and be my friend."

Albert Camus

So, at Jack's two-year-old check-up I broached the subject with Dr. Debra Davis and waited for her to say, "Oh no! He's fine. What soulless, badly dressed half-wit told you to have him tested? *She* should be tested!" She didn't say that. She gave me a flyer and said something like, "Might as well call. It's your tax dollars at work." This marked the beginning of a new phase of my life where I started hearing what "the professionals" said in a new way. The words were one thing, but there was also their inflection, the way their eyes shifted; the *how* of what they said. I was desperate to know what they really thought, because by then I knew there was something wrong with my son, but clung to the hope that someone would say, "No. You're mistaken. He is going to be just fine with a little help."

I revisited conversations in my mind ad nauseam, trying to read between the lines, trying to get clarity, desperate for reassurance. I went for my annual doctor's appointment and mentioned our concerns about Jack. As Dr. Feeney listened, he moved to glance at my file over his shoulder. "What does *that* mean?" I thought. "Does he see something from my pregnancy that could have caused this? Was it the Diet Coke?" Actually, he was just checking to see if I was due for a mammogram.

On August 11, 2004 (my 37th birthday), the First Steps representative arrived to test my son. To see if something was wrong with him. I had asked my sister, Missy, to come.

My vision was that we would share knowing glances with each other throughout the process acknowledging the absurdity of it all. I anticipated all of us laughing at the baselessness of our concern when it was over, and me

Aunt Missy with Jack, 2004.

apologizing to the therapists for having taken their time. "Oh, better safe than sorry!" they would say as they left. You might guess that I always thought these situations would end this way and was continually heartbroken when they didn't.

That was the day I found out that "toe walking," the "pirate eye," visual play (when he held objects off to the side of his head), and intense concentration were markers for autism, as were "flat affect" (a.k.a. permanent resting bitch face), and lack of "reciprocal speech" (conversation). We just thought these were things that made Jack charming. We thought that at the worst he needed some speech therapy. But autism?

Holy shit.

Mari Sandifer

No one was laughing when she left. I can't even recall what Missy and I talked about after the door closed. The truth was that this visit confirmed my worst fear. Something was wrong with Jack that couldn't be fixed and would affect his future and change the trajectory of our family forever. Jack had autism. They did not say it, no one would for years. But if I were honest with myself, I would admit that this was the day I knew it was true.

I didn't know much of anything about autism at that time, the term "autism" conjured up an old TV movie called *Family Pictures* with Kyra Sedgwick.   In the film her character's brother, Randall, was non-verbal, flapped, rocked, and ended up being sent to an institution because he became violent as he got older. One line in the film haunted me: "There is a big difference between a child with autism and a man with autism." I didn't see Jack in this character.

Autism is not a disease. It's not a virus one can catch or a malady that can be cured. I found myself scouring books to find all the reasons Jack was *not* autistic. He didn't have texture issues, he loved to be held, he didn't flap, he didn't line up his toys, he was potty trained, he didn't do this, and he didn't do that. But you see, every autistic person is different from every other one. There's a saying: if you have seen one person with autism, you have seen one person with autism. That is what makes a diagnosis like this so very difficult for a concerned parent to accept. Especially for parents of children who are only mildly affected.

In marketing, they say you must tell a consumer the same thing eight times before they hear you. In my case I had to be pelted with 1,283 glaring examples of how

Jack was different from children whose development was on the fat part of the bell curve, and each time was more heartbreaking than the last.

I learned that autism is a spectrum, like the rainbow, and so it is called autism spectrum disorder (ASD). Some exhibit it more profoundly; no two people exhibit it in the same way. I took countless quizzes online and tallied the scores to see if Jack fell within the spectrum. There was, at the time, a category called "pervasive developmental disorder - not otherwise specified" (PDD-NOS), which was a catch-all for those who were on the spectrum but were very high functioning. Was this like "autism lite"? I am getting anxiety even typing this because it reminds me of the desperation and fear that I felt every minute of every day. And the feeling of isolation. I didn't speak about this with anyone, including Ed. Of course, everyone in the family knew about the testing, but we did not speak about it openly. Putting words to it would make it real. I fantasized that Jack would grow out of it over the next year. I didn't want this damning label, which I likened to a living death sentence attached to my son, until I was absolutely sure. Because you know silly string? You can't put that shit back in the can.

I played games with myself. I figured out how to skew the results of certain quizzes by changing my answers on one or two "borderline" questions. For example, the following questions could go either way with Jack:

- If you point at something across the room does your child look at it?
- Does your child like climbing on things?
- Does your child like to be held?

With these minor tweaks – presto! Jack was *not* on the spectrum. I would then convince myself that I had answered those questions incorrectly the first time. I had been going too fast. Shame on me. But I kept circling back to the characteristic lack of social awareness and interaction among kids with autism. Even as I manipulated the test in my favor, my heart ached as I truthfully answered "no" to the questions that I knew mattered most:

- Does your child play make believe?
- Does your child show interest in other kids?
- Does your child point to show you what he is interested in?

I can see a bit of reference to Kay's concerns as well in a later entry from her journal, dated October 14, 2004. This would have been after the family became aware that we were having jack tested:

Kay's Journal, 2004

Such changes have occurred with Jack. Yesterday we were looking through some of Ed's old toys and found a mixing truck to play with. Jack immediately went to his Bob The Builder Book and located the cement mixer. He may not talk so we can understand him, but he seems to understand a lot!

I saw glaring holes in Jack's social development as he turned two. The nuances of interaction that children learn by simply observing their environment seemed to wash right over Jack. Just when I thought he was catching up, we were closing the gap, I would spend some time with other two-year-old boys and see that the finish line had moved. Exponentially. Yes, he now walked toward the children when they beckoned him as opposed to ignoring them, but then he was unable to join in on whatever they were doing whether it be building a tower with blocks or crashing matchbox cars into each other. On bad days I vacillated between cynicism, irrational panic, and bitterness in my mind. Here's what this looked like:

Cynicism: Yeah. They sure cast a wide net for autism these days! I wonder how much these school systems are taking in from the government? Ed wears glasses. Does that put him on the "blindness spectrum?" Look at me! I'm high-functioning dead!

Irrational Panic: I know we can close this gap if I can just spend every minute in Jack's face. Why is Ed reading the newspaper? That is time wasted that could be spent pulling Jack back from the abyss. Lazy bastard. Must I do *Everything*!?

Bitterness: Is that Monica and Henry? God, I don't need this today. I can't stand that two-year-old verbal freak. But here we are walking toward the church on our way to praise Jesus. I put on my happy mask and approach them. Jack turns from us and walks away to look at something random. Henry looked at me and said, "I like your little boy." That is Jesus speaking through a child. Both convicting and comforting me at the same time, as only He can do. I cried all through church that day.

On good days I opened myself to the possibility, read books, scoured the internet, and cried. All in private. I didn't want to talk about it to anyone. That would make it real.

Denial is the shock absorber for the soul. It protects us until we are equipped to deal with reality.

C.S. Lewis

Chapter 5 – Here Be Dragons

armel, Indiana has over five hundred acres of parkland. Combine that with a bunch of ladies who didn't have children until they were over thirty, throw in a couple of master's degrees and you get a Word document specifying which park we will meet at every Wednesday morning of the summer from ten to noon. You also get a shit-ton of opportunities for me to compare Jack to other little boys his age. Before we had a definite diagnosis, my brain was in overdrive hyper-analyzing Jack's every action and its nuances.

I didn't tell many people that he was being tested, that I was frightened that he had autism, ashamed that it mattered to me, jealous that their kids didn't have it, embarrassed that he didn't act like other kids his age, broken hearted because

Home. Jack's happy place. (And mine), 2006.

the fantasy I had of my life was disappearing, and angry at everyone who didn't have these concerns. I was alone with these thoughts. Isolation was my coping mechanism.

When I stayed at home with Jack, just the two of us, he appeared as "normal" as any other kid. (I would soon learn that "normal' was no longer acceptable in the world of autism. Children who didn't have physical or cognitive or personal difficulties were called "neurotypical." I will use "normal" tongue in cheek throughout this book, so please don't e-mail me.) By this I mean that at home he was just Jack. And we adored him. It was really a combination of two things:

First, we were used to his behavior. The humming, lack of back-and-forth conversation, his need to have things a certain way etc. We simply accommodated him. And there were no typical 2-year-old boys shining a flashlight on his differences. Secondly, home was reliable, and Jack loved it, so he was more relaxed and at his "most normal" there. He knew where his yellow golf club was, how to start a VeggieTales video, where the Cheerios were. The outside world was rife with uncertainties. Golf clubs can get lost, certain houses don't have Cheerios and some kids don't want to watch Bob and Larry. Home was a well-oiled machine.

With each passing week, the social gap seemed to widen. I was terrified. Because the differences were growing larger with time, the fear was, "Will the gap continue to widen? Or will the other kids slow down and give him a chance to catch up?" You know how when you are young a child who is five years older might as well be twenty years older because the difference is so great? But as adults we have friends who are five years older or even twenty, and the difference is no longer there. So, I wondered what the future held for him. Picturing him on a regular school bus, going to middle school, going to high school, being different and left out. My mind reeled, and my heart broke.

I recall a specific day at Cool Creek Park when Jack was three. It had just rained, and Jack had parked himself in the middle of a puddle. And by that, I mean he was standing ankle-deep in mud staring at I don't know what with a serene but distant look on his face. It had started subtly, with just his toes. But I saw what he was doing and knew how it would end because Jack loved gooey things and the puddle looked like chocolate. Our eyes met and I felt like we connected as he inched his way in, and I laughed. Frankly, I just didn't care. His sneakers would wash, and I knew he was going somewhere incredible in his mind.

My friends and their kids were off doing typical things like swinging, going down the slide and playing interactively. I often found myself alone with Jack, but I didn't care. I am an introvert and social activities wear me out. We are similar in that regard. Two mothers I didn't know saw Jack inching his way into the puddle and brought this to my attention, which was weird because I was sitting right there. But I knew the real reason they were saying something. These mothers weren't worried that Jack was messing up his previously white tennis shoes. They were worried that I was letting him do it. Clearly, they had told their "normal" children to stay away from the mud and my parenting choice was making their life difficult.

So, do I ignore them or pretend that his brain is wired like most people's and pull him out? This presented a real dilemma. Here is a handy decision tree:

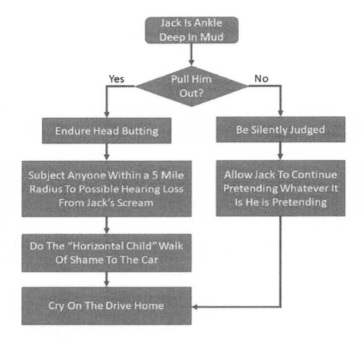

Given that the outcome was going to be the same either way I decided to stay and leave Jack in the mud. Screw them. I hoped they choked on their grande iced sugar-free, vanilla lattes with soymilk. I sat on the ground in front of him to signal to all that *I did, in fact, see him* and studied his face. His beautiful face. "Are you in there?" I asked. He just looked at me. No smile. No connection. But there *was* a connection. In his eyes. I stroked his cheek. You know how something can be so soft that you can't even feel it? His eyes were so light they looked aquamarine under the overcast sky. Everything around me faded away.

When you sense that something is wrong with your child, that he is somehow different, there is a tenderness that grows in your heart. It hurts to be misunderstood and judged by others, but what hurts infinitely more is when others misperceive your child. You become this child's voice. His advocate. He was looking at me with such trust. Out of every person in the world he was looking at me to keep him safe. It was true that he was solitary and preferred to be alone, but when he *did* want someone, that someone was me. The fact that he was so aloof made his desire to be with me all the more precious. Our bond was a coping mechanism God gave me. The obsessive care I felt for Jack was necessary for me to be able to do the work required to be his mom over the next few years. It fueled my creativity,

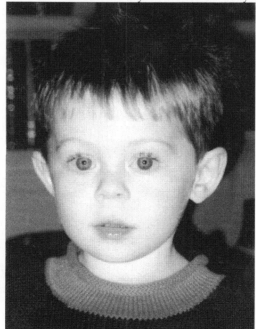

Those eyes. Jack ,2005.

sparked my sense of humor and colored every activity we shared with joy. It still does.

Holding my buddy, 2004.

In years to come I would consider myself lucky to have a child who only wanted to visit a few houses on Halloween before choosing to walk down the street writing down everyone's addresses (in san serif font). I would think "Sucks to be you!" as I drove past the soccer games in 95-degree heat on our way to watch a pipe organ installation. But it was 2005, and I wasn't there yet. Back then I was just so very scared and sad. I wanted to see Jack fit in and act appropriately, but if he was not capable of that, was it unfair to continue to put him in situations that I knew would end badly? This was when I started looking around corners for the boogieman. I didn't want him to catch us unaware. I had to watch for these things and avoid them whenever possible. It was a balancing act, because what ended badly one day might turn out fine in six months as he matured. I started approaching every activity outside of our house with a steely focus that often left me with a headache from clenching my jaw. My focus was on what situation might bring Jack angst or provoke actions by him that would look odd to others or draw attention. Actions like screaming, headbutting or throwing whatever he happened to be holding. I didn't need a winter coat because I was perpetually sweating from adrenaline. I was not in conversations anymore when Jack was around—even as I nodded, my mind was elsewhere. It was exhausting, and yet there was no place I would rather be than with him. I knew that if I gave up on getting out there with him and interacting with the world, we would never taste the victory of an appropriately answered question. I also knew that we would endure the never-ending ways in which a heart can be broken.

There were things that Jack didn't like: loud noises, strong smells, frenetic activity, and crowded rooms. As well as *any* seafood establishment, because those reeked of "pirate smoke." So, all the places that drew most children (museums, water parks, Chuck E. Cheese, Kings Island) were to be avoided. This made me sad on so many levels. Especially when the birthday party invitations arrived. (I didn't know then, that eventually the invitations would just stop arriving.) As I pulled up to one such party Jack had been invited to at the age of five, I saw a school bus that had been converted into a "jumpy fun house obstacle course" kind of thing. "Okay, what kind of fresh hell is this?" I asked myself. If I were who I am now we would have driven right on by and gone directly to Target. But this was back then, and these kids were in Jack's Early Childhood preschool class, so surely whoever was supervising the bus would have some understanding of the signs and ramifications of sensory overload. I left him and went to run a few errands. One stop was at Target (Jack's favorite place to go with me). I bought my requisite large Diet Coke at the snack bar to enjoy on the drive back to pick him up. I deluded myself into believing that he was having the time of his life on the "windowless bouncy bus" and teaching some of his close friends how to do the worm.

I walked into the house and our eyes locked. He spotted the Target cup in my hand (the smoking gun) and went full on feral. I'm certain that given a choice between Target and spending time in the "fun house bouncy obstacle course bus thing" the latter would have come in a distant second. I had ditched him with these loud people and gone to his favorite place *without* him. "Wow. What a *stupid* mistake!" I thought to myself as it all became clear. I don't recall anything besides sitting my cup on the counter, scooping him up and running like hell for my car. I didn't even get his goody bag or say goodbye. Guess where we went?

The only time I left Jack with people who weren't family or from his school was at the nursery during church. I didn't want to do this, but Ed made me, for which I am grateful. However, I never listened to the sermons. I just pictured Jack. Was he missing me? Was he feeling left out? Would they summon us if he was crying? I didn't want over-ambitious nursery Nazis to play hardball with him. After service Ed would laugh as I literally ran to fetch him.

I would do an "IF-THEN" thing in my mind that I

have done since I was a child. As a young girl I played games where IF the light turned green before the end of the song, THEN I would get an Atari for Christmas, or IF the phone stopped ringing after four rings, THEN he would ask me out. Here was the drill, circa 2004:

- IF Jack looks "normal" when I see him at the nursery counter, THEN everything will end up being okay.

- IF Jack notices me and smiles when I get to the nursery counter, THEN everything will end up being okay.

- IF the nursery helper has parted her hair on the right side and is wearing boot cut jeans, THEN everything will end up being okay.

If I could go back and talk to my 37-year-old self I would ask that girl specifically what constituted "everything being okay"? It became more and more difficult to take Jack out in public during this time. Even though he was learning new words every day it was still very difficult for him to make his wishes known, especially under duress. This frustration manifested itself in *a lot* of screaming. When family members would save a seat for Jack and me smack-dab in the middle of a row at one of Betsy's school programs, I was internally saddened and furious at the same time. I had to be able to extricate him from any room STAT if something were to set him off. This helped minimize head-butting (me), hair-pulling (mine), and ear-shattering (everyone's) screams. No way in hell was I going to have to crawl over 23.5 people should one of these episodes arise. Instead I held him on my hip, stood by the door and pitted out whatever shirt I was wearing. "Don't you want to sit down, Mari?" I was asked. *Oh God, if you only knew how much I want to sit down.* But then I would look at Jack, smell his precious head, and there was nowhere else on earth I would rather be.

Finally, I grew to embrace his interests and actually enjoy them to the point that I was *happy* he wasn't on the travelling soccer team. But of course, if he had wanted to play soccer, I would have embraced that too. I feel this is part of having and raising children. The bottom line is that we want our kids to find what it is that makes their heart sing. And then we want to help them develop these interests and take an active part in them.

My brain would eventually compensate and find the silver lining in the ways we spent our time together. I would learn to enjoy what I could enjoy about each situation. For a while I pushed Jack to do things that were expected. I made him play catch, tag, things he had no interest in.

It just took many years for me to give up on the vision I had created in my mind on the day that Jack was born. And it was not a straight line. There were times when I felt I had made peace with all of it, only to feel kicked in the gut by someone's Facebook post about little Tommy finishing his first triathlon…

I would notice boys playing together in groups. I remember driving past a group of three or four middle-school boys walking together down the street. One of them said something and the others burst out laughing. Would I ever see Jack in that situation? Didn't God create us for community? I started envisioning a life of solitude for Jack and it filled me with an overwhelming sadness.

Jack contemplating life, 2007.

My friend, Christopher Thomas, shared an office with me at Ernst & Young. His daughter, Ashley; has spina bifida and was two years old at the time. I was talking to him about these struggles, how it saddened me to watch kids enjoying each other. I worried that Jack would never have this. Then my friend asked a very good question.

"Is Jack happy?" Christopher asked.

"Yes." I answered. He is.

One day after church I looked out the kitchen window at him sitting in the sandbox. The sun was creating a halo on his blond hair. "He will never be lonely a day in his life," I thought. He will never look longingly at a group of boys and wish to be picked because he would rather just watch them. He will never cry at not being invited to the birthday party because he would rather be at home. The party will be loud and confusing. It will take too much energy and will be fraught with the unknown. Why was I mourning the fact that he doesn't have something he doesn't even want? When I was in elementary school my entire class played softball at recess every day. I was terrible at the game and so I started to sit against the fence and just watch. It was heaven for me because I could enjoy watching the game without the stress of having to join in.

To this day whenever I smell freshly cut grass or

Jack enjoying his solitude, 2006.

black tar I am transported back to Wyandotte Elementary School. I wonder what my mother would have felt if she had driven by the school and seen me sitting by myself during recess? Who was I really feeling sorry for? And so, I moved one step in the direction of acceptance. Loosened my grip by one degree. It was a start.

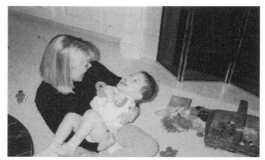

Sharing a good laugh, 2005.

The special needs journey is not one I had planned to take, but I sure do love my tour guide.

Unknown

Chapter 6 – Cue the Angels

The results of the First Step testing that took place in August of 2004 indicated that Jack qualified for speech and occupational therapy. The name of the second one confused me, but apparently Jack's "occupation" was to be a two-year-old boy, so the occupational therapist would work with him to succeed in things like playing appropriately, changing tasks without going ballistic, coloring, and other things two-year-old's typically did. The women that came to discuss the results never used the word "autism." They just showed me Jack's score for different measures and how he faired next to neurologically typical kids his age.

I was in shock, still believing that they would tell me mainstream preschool was all it would take to bring him up to speed. I looked through a list of therapists and picked a couple who seemed... well, actually, I have no idea why I picked the ones I did, but Baby Jesus must have sent the two women I chose because they were both angels. One of them, Renee Alberts, remains a friend to this day. They both came to our house on Mondays and Wednesdays to work with Jack. I worked from home on those days and sat at the kitchen island so I could hear how they were interacting with him and would be able to replicate the approach 24/7. I am nothing if not tenacious. I was determined to learn what they did, teach Ed and Betsy the best ways to draw Jack out, and as a family we would blitzkrieg these ASD tendencies. We could take all of those pesky autism markers and nip things right in the bud. Kick some big autism ass. Go team Sandifer!

As tortuous as this period was, I have some truly wonderful and poignant memories from the therapy days. These talented women taught me the mysteries of the human brain, miraculous things that I never learned in business school. Barbara, the occupational therapist, put a toy in front of Jack to the side. She was thrilled when he used his dominant hand and reached across his midline to retrieve it. Crossing the midline (the middle of his body) is an important prerequisite for development of many motor and cognitive skills. It is as fundamental for reaching other learning and developmental steps as developing sustained attention or the ability to self-regulate. Who knew?

Renee, the speech therapist, showed Jack a flash card with a cat on it, pronounced the word "cat" for him and then a few minutes later asked him what it was. She was happy that he referred to it as a kitten; as Jack tended to parrot other people's words rather than use his own. The meaningless repetition of another person's spoken words is common among children with autism. When Jack brought her a book for the first time, she commented that this meant he was developing the ability to seek out an adult for the purpose of sharing enjoyment with another person. This was really good stuff! These ladies always arrived with wonderful toys that Jack loved, with the goal of getting him to engage in reciprocal play. That is, exchanging thoughts and responses with another person and playing cooperatively.

These sessions were sometimes as therapeutic for me as they were for Jack. I had been so alone in my worry about him that they provided healing moments of adult friendship with talented women who knew what I was feeling and facing. But there were days when we simply decided to put autism on the shelf, and those were some of the best. Renee taught Betsy and me how to play the dreidel game. She is Jewish, and I didn't know about Google yet, so we needed her to teach us. She was also there the day my newly reupholstered sofa was delivered and loved the trim I had used for the throw pillows.

Certain days stick out in my mind because of the way the heavens opened, and God gave me a wink. On one of those days, Renee corrected Jack on the way he was trying to assemble a set of train tracks she had brought. He moved on to play with something else and came back to the tracks later. She was thrilled when he started to do the task incorrectly again, caught himself, and did it the correct way that she had shown him. It was exciting to see him begin to self-monitor and change based on what he was taught. This demonstrated his ability to be less self-directed and less rigid, or routine driven. He enjoyed positive feedback which kept him engaged in learning new things.

These were all such hopeful signs. Truly reasons for celebration. But I continued to struggle accepting an autistic son as my reality. At the end of each of Barbara's and Renee's sessions, they filled out a form for Jack's file. I would read it after they left, looking for the part where it said "Jack seems to be fine now. Truly a miraculous recovery. His mother is a Godsend and should be portrayed by Reese Witherspoon in the Lifetime made-for-TV movie about the mother who discovers a cure for autism…"

But I never saw that. I would read these reports several times throughout the day, as if those phrases were really there and I had simply missed them before. I felt like I was losing my mind. During 2004 and 2005 I read every book I could find on autism. I scoured the internet and cried in my cubicle at work. I watched Jack's every move, and the moves of every other two-year-old boy I encountered. And my heart hurt. As I learned more about the spectrum, this knowledge did not bring empowerment. Not at first. It was a dark time made darker by isolation, fear, and sadness.

I could not watch home movies of Betsy older than twelve months because the differences between the two in their verbal development and social abilities were glaring. It wasn't that I wanted Jack to be as outgoing and "Shirley Temple-esque" as Betsy had been. I loved that he was more of a cool customer. My fear was that he wasn't *choosing* to stare blankly at the annoying person who was trying to engage him, but that he was *not able or even aware* that he was supposed to respond. As an introvert, I know how much energy it takes to be responsive and engaged when it doesn't come naturally. I hoped that he was just introverted and choosy with regard to whom he wanted to spend his energy on. But I was also worried that he was not all there and never would be.

All the things Jack did and didn't do were the things that made him Jack. And I simply adored this precious boy. No diagnosis would change who he was, which was a little boy who had stolen my heart. So why was I so tormented? What was I afraid of? I believe for me the hardest part was living with the unknown. We just didn't know what Jack would be in the coming years. I had to admit my true fears to myself. From worst to best case, these fears were:

- Jack was cognitively impaired and would never be able to communicate, which meant he would never be able to live independently.

- Jack was actually very smart but would never develop social skills and would always be seen as "strange" by people who didn't know him.

- Jack was very intelligent and would catch up socially, becoming a successful man, a snappy dresser with a whip-smart sense of humor.

These were very real concerns. The concern for how others perceive our children is always there, as much as we wish it weren't. I knew the high road was to not care. But alas, I did care. I do care. There is a scene in the movie *Hope Floats*. In it, Sandra Bullock's character and her daughter have moved back in with her mom (Gena Rowlands) after Sandra's husband leaves her. Sandra's nephew is also living there, and he is, in a word, strange. Instead of speaking, he communicates by barking. In one scene he has dressed himself like a frog. It's not Halloween, he just dressed up for no reason. What I loved, though, was that his grandmother acted like he was completely normal, frog suit or not. "Right, Travis?" she says to him in one scene. "Yes. He knows! It's not easy being green."

In the end, I knew my peace would only come when I decided that I could live a glorious and blessed life no matter which scenario played out. But in the fall of 2004, that was a distant goal. One Sunday night after everyone had gone to sleep and as I watched *Mad Men*, I listed all of the things Jack did that made him look autistic.

- Humming for no good reason.

- Carrying a plastic golf club. Everywhere.

- Slapping himself when he was angry.

- Not calling me Mommy but calling Ed and me the same thing. A hybrid mashup: "mommydaddy."

- Responding to questions with a "Jackie Kennedy stare" or with answers that made no sense.

- Not playing with other kids.

- Wanting to play alone.

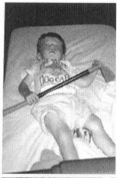

The Famed Yellow Putter – It went EVERYWHERE.

I looked at each one and tried to figure out how I could get him to stop doing that. But if I did, would he start doing other, even weirder, things? Things that would make me nostalgic for the yellow putter?

There were good days and bad, and it was always shocking to me how suddenly and unexpectedly waves of grief and fear could be dredged up on an otherwise happy day. I remember a trip to Target with Betsy and Jack. We were walking through the toy section and I overheard a boy Jack's age in the next aisle begging for some item. His mother was getting exasperated and threatening to leave the store. I looked at Jack. His eyes scanned the endless selection of toys, but his expression didn't change. "He doesn't know to ask for a toy, or to point to one he wants," I thought. "He's almost three. Does he even recognize that these are toys?"

He did play with toys at home, but now that I thought about it, he also loved drink stirrers, sugar packets, and Grandma Kay's wine stopper. On the previous Christmas, Betsy had to open Jack's presents for him because he didn't understand what he was supposed to do and wasn't even interested. Instead of playing with his "real" toys, he carried around a large Chinet plate all day saying, "Oval. Oval. Oval." The fear I felt bordered on terror. "Oh my God," I thought. "We have to teach him how to play with toys!" This became my new mission. I feel so sorry for that girl as I write this. She wears me out.

She ran without stopping. Feverishly trying to fix it; not knowing that it was already perfect.

Mari Sandifer

Chapter 7 – For Whom the Bell Curve Tolls

In 2004, Indiana First Step benefits only covered a child until his or her third birthday. At that point, if services were still needed, the child could qualify for the Developmental Preschool offered by their school district. For us, that was the Carmel Clay Schools, and a test was required. I love a good test. Go ahead. Test my personality, love language, spiritual gifts, enneagram--I love them all. I was up for Jack being tested again to see if he would qualify for the developmental preschool because I was fairly certain that he would *not* qualify. His vocabulary was growing by leaps and bounds. He wasn't as social as his sister, but since when does being introverted equate with being autistic? It would be time to graduate from these therapies and move on, recalling this past year like one remembers a year studying for the CPA exam. Difficult, beneficial, and over.

Jack's test was scheduled to take place at our house on the Wednesday morning before Thanksgiving, 2004. We were told it would take about three hours, so we arranged for Ed's parents to pick up Betsy from kindergarten. Ed stayed home. I don't recall the name of the woman who came, but she was very kind. Let's call her Sue. Sue spent time alone with Jack, alone separately with Ed and me, and with us as a couple, asking questions and making observations. I found myself becoming more and more anxious, defensive, and agitated as the hours passed. I could see and hear Jack falling short. Not knowing what a button was or where orange juice came from. Not responding. Responding inappropriately. My brain buzzed, "SHIT! I forgot to teach him what a button is! We'll do that tonight."

I was in the laundry room eavesdropping on Ed as he answered Sue's questions.

Sue asked, "Does Jack notice when others are upset?"

"Yes! YES! He does notice. And he feels deeply," I thought to myself.

"Not usually," Ed says. "Especially if he is concentrating on something else."

I screamed from the laundry room, "That's not TRUE! He gets upset when Betsy cries. He *screams* when she's upset."

"Oh yes," Ed says, "You're right. He does do that."

Bastard. He is making Jack look bad.

My brain spiraled into full-on lizard mode and things went downhill from there. Ed answered another question "wrong" and I completely lost it. "You're not giving him credit. You are forgetting all that he can do!" Ed was now angry and defensive, but Sue looked at me with compassion. I could tell she was not shocked or offended or embarrassed for me. She had seen this before.

Literally minutes before Betsy and my parents-in-law would come back, Sue handed me a chart and told me that by her scoring Jack had an IQ of 67. I'm a business major so this meant nothing to me. Was that like a 67%? A grade of D? That wasn't so bad. It wasn't an F. I looked down at the chart and realized that it was bell curve with IQs down the left and unfamiliar mnemonics down the right side. I found 67 on the left and followed it with my red fingernail across the page. My finger landed on MMR. "What is MMR?" I asked.

Silence for a moment. Then Sue said, "Mildly Mentally Retarded."

I was shocked to hear that the word "retarded" was being used in this day and age under any circumstance, but especially in relation to my son. I dropped my face into my hands and cried. My head felt like it weighed a thousand pounds. Even when I heard Jim, Kay, and Betsy walking into the kitchen I couldn't lift it. When I finally did, I saw Jim sitting quietly at the kitchen table with his head down. Kay was directly behind him staring out the window. She had her hand resting on his shoulder. She looked like she was in shock. Neither was looking in our direction.

Sue went on to qualify all of this by stating what now is better known. Children who have speech delays cannot be accurately tested for IQ. They are guaranteed to bomb the test. Wait. Did she say speech delay? That's not autism. I liked the sound of that. Can we take that diagnosis instead? Sue listed three possible scenarios: Jack had speech delays that would work themselves out over time; Jack had autism; or Jack had autism and was also cognitively impaired. My mind was circling the vortex of despair and grabbing wildly for any shred of hope. "The first one. I'll take choice number one. Just tell me what we need to do to make that one happen."

Ed asked Sue when we would know what we were dealing with. She told us that we would just need to watch him closely over the next few years. Excuse me? Three years? As in thirty-six months? I must live with this uncertainty past today? I thought today was the day we would finally know the truth. After the hellish rollercoaster ride of the past twelve months I was certain that adding 1,095 more days of uncertainty to this nightmare and folding in the possibility of "MMR" would send me directly to the booby hatch. As Sue prepared to leave, she told Ed to "take good care of your wife." I loved her for saying that. She recognized a woman on a ledge when she saw one.

It's strange, but after Sue left Ed's parents said nothing about what they had witnessed. They didn't ask what Sue had said or come at us with hugs and tears. This turned out to be a gift. We all had to process what was going on in our own heads. As a group we didn't talk about the elephant in the room and Ed never shunned me for being so rude to him. I'm pretty sure we were all just in shock.

Plus, Betsy was back. She had chosen something from the book fair for Jack: a set of nine thin books representing each of the (then) nine planets. Oh, that joyful, thoughtful, girl. After what we had just been through, seeing her was like feeling the warmth of the sun on my face. And Jack adored those books almost as much as he adored his big sister. Betsy's relationship with her brother was and is truly special. I have to wonder where he would be today had we not had the gift of Betsy in our home. It takes energy, commitment, and tenacity to get a child on the spectrum to "play" with you. I might join Jack on the floor and run my matchbox car into his only to be met with Jack simply getting up and walking away. Often, we would start a game of family hide-and-seek only to find Jack looking at a book

***Falling asleep reading his book fair gift from Betsy
(Pluto was robbed), 2005.***

in the basement, having decided to stop playing. Truth
be told, it is much easier to walk away and read *People*
magazine than it is to continue the quest for interactive
play with kids like this because they truly just want to be
left alone. But Jack was young, so we could affect how his
brain worked, we could give him new neural pathways, so
giving up wasn't an option. We wanted to expose him to
as much social interaction as possible so that he could find
joy in this world.

We live in a relational world. My default is to be alone,
especially when things are hard, but the true God moments
happen when I allow others in, when I allow myself to
be vulnerable. I wanted Jack to see how much fun playing
with another person could be, and Betsy was that person
for Jack. She still is. As I write this, I can hear her upstairs
talking to Jack about his day at school and messing with
him. It is funny to be typing these stories as I listen to them
as teenagers now. Jack is 16 and Betsy is 19. She is asking
what he is looking at on his laptop and threatening to

Mari Sandifer

come see. Jack has taken to looking at images of animated characters from Disney movies and Betsy likes to tease him about it. While some teenagers' parents are horrified by a Google search history that includes pornographic terminology, my laptop history includes: "Pongo runs away" and "Brenda Blue is dancing." He escapes into a world that boys his age have left behind. Betsy draws him out of that world and back into ours like no other. She was and remains the most extraordinary woman I know. And she has always been able to bring out his joy in a beautiful way. But when Betsy was five, we did not discuss any of our concerns with her. We didn't tell her at the time that Jack was being tested, or that his brain worked differently. But we didn't have to. She intuitively knew that he needed extra guidance. She understood that when he found a game he liked they would have to play it over and over and over and over and over again. And she never complained or showed frustration with him.

In this Christmas picture taken with Santa Claus, you can see on Betsy's face that even while she is looking at Ed and me, she's also aware of Jack's growing discomfort and is trying to reassure him. You can tell by the angle of

Betsy on high alert, 2005.

her head that she had been looking at him one millisecond earlier, most likely telling him to smile for the camera. And her eyes are reassuring us too: "Yes, he could blow at any minute, but I will take care of it." I have seen this look on her face countless times over the years. She has the ability to model social behavior for Jack while respecting his differences. To encourage and correct him without making him feel ashamed or embarrassed. This spirit of discernment and ability to multitask during stressful situations cannot be taught. It is a gift. And Betsy has it.

Mari Sandifer

If you want to know how your girl will treat you after marriage, just listen to her talking to her little brother.

Sam Levenson

Chapter 8 – He's IN THERE!

And so, after the test, I waited. I watched. I wanted to see something that indicated synapses were firing. At this point my fears went beyond autism. Now there was the possibility that Jack was also cognitively impaired. Before, I was just worried about Jack seeming "odd" and being unable to sustain friendships. Now I had visions of him never graduating from high school. God help me, it mattered that Jack be smart. And funny. I wanted him to have these gifts. I felt like more and more of the things I had envisioned for Jack were being stripped away. I thought of kids with cancer who would not live to go to middle school, and I felt guilty for wanting Jack to be able to learn and laugh with his friends. I had a very limited view on what intelligence and friendship meant back then.

I was on high alert in every way. Once while driving I was sure that a semi just up ahead had "autism solutions" on its side with an 800 number. "Thank God!" I thought, as I sped up to jot the number down. I pulled up alongside and reality took over. "Audio Solutions."

Oh. Never mind.

I was still looking for reasons that Jack was "normal." And if not that, I was looking for ways in which he could be "made normal." The fact that I was having visions while driving indicated that I was spinning.

As I read books about autism, I recognized my childhood self in some of the descriptions. "Maybe I would have been diagnosed as a child if they had used the same criteria then," I thought. "Maybe he will grow out of this and be just fine. You know! Like *me*?" I had heard that Einstein used to get lost going home because he lived in a townhouse and they all looked the same. We were living in a townhouse when I began to write this book. They all looked the same to me. One night I accidentally opened the front door of our next-door neighbor. Luckily, I instantaneously realized my error and backed out before anyone noticed. I can be smart in certain instances but incredibly clueless in others. Maybe I'm on the autism spectrum somewhere? Thus, my mind took one more turn on the hamster wheel.

One thing that saddened me during this time was that I still couldn't get Jack to have a conversation. I could get him to go back and forth maybe twice with one-word answers, but then the wheels would fall off. For example:

Me: Jack, where are we going?

Jack: Get Betsy.

Me: Where is she?

Jack: Peacock.

Shit.

After I received the troubling IQ rating in November, these failed conversations concerned me even more. I was on the lookout for any sign of cognitive ability and was happy to see evidence in this area as we prepared for Jack to start preschool. Children on the spectrum are very concrete thinkers, which is why they gravitate to concrete things like numbers and shapes and facts. When Betsy started to draw it was usually pictures of people, houses, pets; and the like. They were relational pictures that reflected the activities that people engage in. Jack drew objects and became obsessed with planets, colors, numbers, letters and shapes.

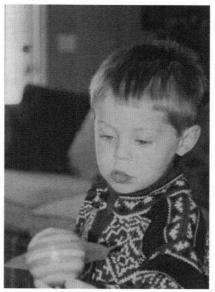

Saturn was his favorite with all those fancy rings, 2004.

The Arby's Restaurants in Indiana have red and white square tiles on the outside of their buildings. The tradition was that as I approached the drive-through, Jack would scream, "Square! Square! Square!" Then one day we had pulled up to Arby's and he began the expected shouts of "Square! Square!" But this afternoon there was a pause and I heard him say quietly, as if to himself, "Diamond." What? I looked in my rear-view mirror and saw him looking at the building. His head was cocked at a forty-five degree angle.

Betsy had received a game for her fourth birthday called

Colorama. It was filled with squares, circles, pentagons, trapezoids and triangles, each one in the colors of blue, green, red and yellow. I don't recall who in the family made this discovery, but if you asked Jack to find the blue trapezoid he could. It was the same with every possible color/shape combination. He never got it wrong. I never taught shapes and colors to Jack, nor did Betsy or Ed. He must have gotten it from books we read to him or from the television. I was too busy trying to teach him what a button was.

When I showed this trick to his speech therapist, Renee, it was one of those Lifetime made-for-TV moments. We screamed and clapped. My vision was that now everything would turn around. This would be the moment we would always remember as when we had finally "broken through." That even if Jack was on the spectrum, he was exceptional in his own way.

It felt like a veil was being lifted. I was starting to accept that Jack was different, but also finding joy in the ways he was different. These were the things that made me start to question my obsession with the fat part of the bell curve. Maybe being an outlier wasn't so bad? I found myself wanting Jack to be the wacky genius. At times he did things far beyond his age, while in the next minute I found myself running to stop him from dropping trou in Lowe's to pee in a display toilet. The extremes gave me whiplash. But they also made me look at the human brain with wonder.

Jack didn't say much, so it was easy to assume that nothing was going on in his head, that there might not be anything "there." I never tried to teach him the traditional things one would teach a three-year-old, because, frankly, I just wanted him to call me Mom. One day I heard singing coming from below. I realized that Jack was in the basement singing the ABCs with a toy. I sneaked down and got video of this because it was just so darn cute.

I thought he had memorized the song by hearing it and that he probably didn't even know that he was singing letters, or that letters were even a thing, for that matter. But as I got closer, I noticed a long string of letters on the floor beside him placed closely together like a curving train. It was the alphabet. In order. I hadn't taught him this.

Jack's alphabet train, 2005.

The summer that Jack was three we took a trip to Hilton Head Island. I was pushing him in the stroller, and he was holding one of those types of Frisbees that have no middle. Like a big O. He liked to carry it because it was a circle. We tried to get him to throw it and play Frisbee in the traditional sense and I was always disappointed that he never wanted to. On this day I noticed him put it over his head as if he were going to wear it like a necklace. Except that he just held it there, not lowering it to his neck as I had expected. Is he using it as a crown?

I asked him, "What are you doing?"

"I'm Saturn," he said.

Planets were always special to him, especially since Betsy had gotten him the set of planet books from the book fair. I had always comforted myself when Jack didn't exhibit certain traditional autistic traits, thinking he was therefore "less autistic" and perhaps more likely to grow out of this troubling phase. One of these traits was putting objects into lines for no reason that made sense. For example, any child will line up their cars and that makes sense because perhaps they are making a parking lot or a traffic jam. A child on the spectrum might line up their socks on the floor and *freak out* if you move one. I was very proud that Jack never did that. Then one day, as I came into the family room, I saw his planet books neatly lined up on the floor. The wind was knocked out of me. *"Oh, dear God, no,"* I thought. But then I stopped and looked again. I noticed Pluto was last, and then I saw that earth was the third one

Jack's planet train, 2005.

in. I don't know the order of the planets. I never have. But I do know that Pluto is last, and that earth is third (I know this from watching the nineties sitcom *Third Rock from the Sun*) I grabbed another of his many planet books and compared the solar system diagram to his "planet train." They were in the correct order. Neither Ed, Betsy, nor I had done anything with Jack that would teach him this.

I also began to see glimmers of his sense of humor. One memory sticks out as if it were yesterday. I was getting ready to take Betsy to swimming lessons at Stoney Creek. Jack was standing at the couch intently looking at one of his planet books when I called him to come over so I could put his shoes on. As usual, he didn't comply or even acknowledge that I was speaking to him. I stood there and implored him a second and then a third time to come to me. Without looking away from his book, he simply lifted his left leg out to the side and in my direction. *Oh my God*, I thought, he is messing with me. And is that a smirk? *Sweet baby Jesus in a manger.* He is messing with me and knows it is funny. I grabbed him and tickled him until he laughed so hard, he got the hiccups.

And with this sense of humor returned the glorious lights that had been missing from his eyes. In a very short period of time he became downright wacky, which delighted me to no end. It was as if someone had flipped a switch and his personality was back.

Mari Sandifer

You keep that "cure" of yours. I'll keep my brilliant and quirky child and we'll call it even.

Autism Sparkles

Chapter 9 – Sophie's Choice

As a result of Jack's testing at Thanksgiving, he was accepted into the Carmel Clay School System's Developmental Preschool, a preschool especially designed for children with special needs, physical or developmental. This is not like being accepted to Dalton, and I still hoped that after the first day I would receive a call: "There has been a huge mistake. What dumbass told you that your son belonged here? Please pick him up immediately and take him to the Park Tudor Preparatory School, where a full ride scholarship awaits."

The Carmel Lutheran preschool Betsy had attended had a place reserved for Jack. This thrilled us because they also had a lengthy waiting list. So, we were met with a dilemma: Do we send him to the preschool for typically developing kids and hope that this is just a phase he will grow out of? The school's literature said it could accommodate one to two children with disabilities in their class. Did Jack count as disabled by their criteria? This could be like AB testing in the marketing world: we could send him in and see if they notice anything. Maybe when we tell people that he was being watched for autism it skews how they see him. If he could pass for normal, maybe he actually is or could be if that's how they treated him …? My mind went on and on, ad nauseam. Fire up that trusty hamster wheel. Every. Day.

I wanted to pretend for a couple more years that this was something that would work itself out. Sending him to special ed preschool was not a bell that could be unrung in my mind. And yet what if I was allowing my pride to get in the way of putting Jack in an environment richly equipped to draw out his best and prepare him for kindergarten?

In addition, there was the Diane Knollman consideration, which could not be ignored. Diane had been Betsy's preschool teacher at the Lutheran preschool and had since moved to the Carmel Clay school system's Early Childhood Program. In one of my worried moments, I had reached out to her via email. Her response was swift and compassionate. She told me that she was so sorry we had been going through what she knew to be a frightening and sad time. So, if we did send Jack to the Developmental Preschool, in an ironic twist, he would end up having this sympathetic soul as his teacher, just as Betsy had.

When I consider the thoughts and opinions I had regarding developmental preschool in 2005, I wouldn't exactly call myself a jackass; but I wouldn't exactly call myself anything else, either. I knew that having these options for Jack was a gift, but I wondered if there was any way we could whistle past the graveyard and have everything turn out not only good, but so good as to be a riveting anecdote shared at the reception we would host to celebrate his graduation from MIT. And so, on a drizzly gray day in February 2005, I drove to visit each school. We had to decide pronto because there was a waiting list for both schools and I wanted this to be a great day for another family out there who would receive one of these spots.

My first stop was at the Carmel Clay Developmental Preschool. Diane Knollman came to the front desk to get me after I signed in. God bless this precious woman. She led me down the hall and into the brightly lit, beautifully appointed room equipped with all manner of synapse-firing toys and teaching tools. My eyes ricocheted from child to child. The first had Down syndrome, the second was wearing a sensory vest, which is a tightly fitting vest around the torso meant to help calm a restless child. (He must be on the autism spectrum, I thought.), a third was having some type of meltdown in the corner and being tended to by an aide.

I knew that the Developmental Preschool had a couple of "normal" kids in each class who got to attend free as "peer facilitators." These were usually siblings of kids who had been through the program, which was how they had come to know about the opportunity. I found myself eyeing each child as if trying to spot a fake Gucci. Who are the moles? I wanted to find the peer facilitator children to see if Jack looked more like one of them. Could he maybe be a hybrid? Perhaps they would develop an "assistant to the peer facilitator" role for Jack because clearly, he wasn't as disabled as the children I was seeing here. Did my son really belong *here*?

Next stop was the "preschool for normal children." I had decided not to send Jack incognito, so I spoke to one of the admission directors. "I wanted to let you know that while we don't have a formal diagnosis, our son is being evaluated for autism spectrum disorder. I read that you can only accommodate a couple of kids with disabil--" I could not finish the word and my voice cracked. There was an awkward silence and I couldn't look up because gravity would have pulled the tears down. I blinked and one fell directly on the table I was leaning over. The woman touched my arm and said with such compassion, "I am sure Jack will do just fine here." I made a beeline for my car so that I could commence with the ugly cry in private. I was thankful for the forty-minute drive to my job downtown.

I couldn't help but see it as a God thing that if Jack were to attend the Developmental Preschool, his teacher would be the very woman who had taught Betsy and who had been so considerate earlier that year. So, in the end, we decided to send Jack to the Developmental Preschool. Anything else felt like setting him up for failure while denying him help from people who had dedicated their lives to working with these extraordinary children. But even after we had made peace with this decision, my mind went into a state of second-guessing overdrive.

Here is a typical stream of consciousness from that time:

- Perhaps the "normal" children will be a good influence and give him examples of appropriate play and behavior.

- Will the children who are more affected by autism model the very behaviors that we are trying to eliminate?

- If he goes there everyone will *know* something is wrong. It will be real.

- Would the peer facilitator kids take Jack under their wing and give him special one-on-one attention? That could be cool! Maybe their moms would even invite Jack over for a playdate because isn't preschool where kids make their first friends?

- Note to self: Jack is really a cute kid. I'll have to go to the Fashion Mall and spend an offensive amount of money on clothes from Baby Gap. If he's going to act weird at least he'll look super-adorable while doing it.

(Pause to take a refreshing sip from inverted water bottle. Jump right back on that hamster wheel.)

These are the thoughts that looped 25/8 during February 2005. When a child opts into this program, they can start as soon as they turn three. Jack's third birthday was Sunday, April 10, 2005. So, I scheduled him to start on Monday, April 11.

"Why not just wait to start him in the fall?" I used to hear. Silly people. Clearly, they didn't understand about the plasticity of the toddler brain. The brain essentially rewires itself and adjusts its own "geography" as a response to changes in environment. Thinking, acting, and learning result in significant changes to the brain's physical structure and function. Plasticity is exponentially greater in young children. That's why it is so much easier to teach a five-year-old a second language than a fifty-year-old. Waiting until the fall would mean missing thirty-two glorious days of early intervention. Then there was the possibility of summer school. He could be totally cured by next fall!

I have vivid recollections of God meeting me where I was during this season and making his presence abundantly clear. After we had decided to enroll Jack in the Developmental Preschool program, I had to drop off a copy of his birth certificate to Prairie Trace Elementary, where the Preschool was located. After I signed in at the front desk, I made my way to Diane's room.

This happened to be the day mothers were dropping off items for a fundraising bake sale scheduled for the weekend. One thing I was not up to on this day was interacting with ridiculous mothers of "normal children" wearing Lululemon's and toting homemade peanut-and-gluten-free iced cookies in the shape of the school mascot. I quickly turned and beat a hasty retreat to a back hall that was deserted. As I walked, I looked down because my eyes were burning with tears. Then I heard footsteps coming toward me. I looked up. It was Diane Knollman. She met my gaze with a warm smile and greeted me with a hug. Yes. This was the person who should be Jack's preschool teacher. This is the right place for him. Jack would attend the Carmel Clay Developmental Preschool.

The LORD himself goes before you and will be with you; He will never leave you nor forsake you. Do not be afraid; do not be discouraged.

Deuteronomy 31:8

Chapter 10 – Oh Short Bus, My Short Bus

The peace I felt with this decision was palpable. But there were still decisions to be made. Would I drive him every day or allow the short bus to pick him up? At first blush the answer was easy. Short bus? HELL. NO. In the 1980s we used to call the short bus "the tard cart." I know. Hideous. It horrifies me as much to type it as it does for you to read it.

Don't forget, at this time I still believed this was all a mistake. If it turned out as I expected, I didn't want the stench of the short bus wafting off my boy as he entered elementary school. It seemed a no-brainer. Until I spoke with Diane. She told me emphatically that the bus often turned out to be the most exciting element of school for the children. She said that when asked about their favorite part of school, most kids said it was riding the bus.

I don't know how she changed my mind so quickly, because I cared so much what other people thought of me and mine back then. I can only believe that God flipped a switch in my brain, because in the blink of an eye I was fully on board. Ed said it was my call. He says that a lot and it is one of the things I love most about him. If Jack would like the bus and not give a rat's ass that it was short, then I, too, could make my peace. To this day my heart smiles when I see one of those little buses tool past. I always say a quick prayer for the kids, their families, and their teachers.

Mari Sandifer

I could not have known then the role school buses would play in our lives for several years to come. We would spend hours drawing them, cutting them out, counting the windows, listing bus numbers, playing hide and seek on them (back then they left them unlocked over the weekend and all parked together in one lot, but as of 2019, there is a restrictive gate). More about buses later...

When I watch video from Jack's third birthday, I can only feel sorry for the me that I see, because all I was thinking about during that party was that my son was starting special ed the next day. A short bus for children with special needs was going to come to our house and pull into our driveway. For my son. I was going to put my little boy on that bus and let it drive away with him. What would he be thinking as it pulled away from me and took him to an unfamiliar place filled with people he didn't know? He will be scared. And sad. He will wonder how and why I allowed this to happen. And he will wonder how long it will last, what activity is coming next. Where his yellow putter is. And when he will see me again. Children like Jack

Jack's third birthday, April 10, 2005.

thrive on routine and familiarity. He was going somewhere that didn't hold one shred of anything familiar. And I was going to let this happen.

"Oh, Jack, please forgive me. I wish you could just stay here with me forever and we could snuggle on the couch and watch *VeggieTales*. I don't care if you don't learn to talk properly, because I always know what you want. It could just be you and I. We never have to leave because my favorite place is with you. Just us."

But of course, I knew that couldn't be. The world is a big and glorious place. Jesus loves us too much to leave us the way we are. He allows us to be stretched by this life and we are better people for it. So, I had to let him go. Video of us putting him on the bus breaks my heart because you can hear him protesting as the door shuts. Betsy can't watch it to this day.

After the bus backed out of the driveway, Ed continued to film for about ten seconds. There is no sound. Neither of us said anything or even looked at each other. And then the film fades out. As I walked into the kitchen the Holy Spirit gave me a gift. I had a flash of memory from a movie about Ray Charles. In one scene he is a child and has just lost his vision. He runs through the kitchen and trips. As he lies on the ground he cries out for his mother, but she never comes. He cries and yells again as he crawls along trying to find his way. It's truly gut-wrenching to watch. Yet, in time he finds his bearings and rises to his feet victoriously. You can see the realization wash across his face, the synapses firing—the knowledge that he *does* have the ability to help himself. It's only then that the camera pans to his mother, who is sitting in the corner just five

Monday, April 11, 2005.

feet away, crying softly as she witnesses his struggle but choosing to hold back. She had been there the whole time, loving him enough to allow the suffering that would end in victory. As she watched she didn't know how it would end, but she knew that stepping in would rob him of something more valuable: the possibility of victory. That's the rub. I wonder how often God does that for me?

Diane phoned me that afternoon, as she does on the

first day for every new mom. Yes, he had cried all the way to school. But a little girl with Down syndrome named Mackenzie took his hand and held it the entire way. I wept at hearing this. I wept over my own ignorance and pride. I wept as I asked Diane to please let that little girl's mother know that she is raising a tender-hearted child. I wept as I looked across the room at Jack and knew that he was exactly where he was supposed to be. I wept because I knew Diane loved Jack almost as much as I did. I wept because Jesus is ever faithful, and His fingerprints were all over this.

Mari Sandifer

His compassions never fail. They are new
every morning; great is His faithfulness.
Lamentations 3:22-23

Mari Sandifer

Chapter 11 – The Preschool Years

What I remember most vividly about the preschool years was the uncertainty and fear. Every child in elementary or secondary school with a disability identified in law is given an IEP, Individualized Educational Plan, which is developed to ensure that the child receives specialized instruction and related services. At one of these meetings I asked the counselor if Jack would ever be able to hold a coherent conversation.

Her answer was, "I don't know."

"*Wow*," I thought. "*That blows.*"

Yet we saw so much growth. For instance, one day when Jack was four, Diane called me at work. "Mari, you won't believe what I am witnessing right now. Olivia is playing house, and Jack is being the baby! She just fed him a bottle! He just pretended to cry for more." This was grade-A reciprocal play at a level we had never witnessed in him before. I sent her this email in response that indicates we were also seeing exciting things at home.

Hello Diane -

> God love that little Olivia. Ed and I have also seen some jaw-dropping activities from Jack lately in the social department. It makes my heart soar to see him enjoy other children and I have shed a few tears myself watching him interact with the

neighborhood kids from our kitchen window this last week. Thank you for your enthusiasm and love you have for our precious son. You'll never know how much it meant to me that you called to share this good report. I will never forget it.

Mari

Kay watched Jack in the afternoons because preschool was only in the mornings. She had continued with her own journal:

From Kay's Journal, dated May 3, 2005:

So much is happening in Jack's life. Jack is talking more. He is not crying and screaming like he used to. He sits at the table and eats with us. This week we took him to Starbucks, and he loved his cinnamon roll. Today we were watching the DVD Galileo and the stars came up. He called them "Starbucks" and laughed. I love his sense of humor.

When I look at the birthday letter we wrote for Jacks fourth birthday, I see the development of a keen sense of humor as well:

April 10, 2006: You have developed quite a sense of humor this last year. Your favorite joke is to change the words of songs or provide nonsense answers to obvious questions. For example, when we drop Betsy off at piano lessons you think it's quite hilarious to declare that she has gone to Sunday school or is at gymnastics class. You are also the master of play-on-words like changing a line in Blue's Clues from "Get your handy-dandy note pad" to "Get your handy-mommy note pad" and then you laugh so hard that you get the hiccups. We also have a game where you pretend to cry and say, "I'm so crying!" – then you start to laugh. You also enjoy going to McDonalds and playing on the slides. You climb up with the agility of a monkey and your laughter can he heard as you make your way down the tube slide. I have a winter jacket that has a black, faux fur collar that you absolutely LOVE. You call it your "soft coat" and request it on a daily basis. Apparently, the soft fur feels delightful on your little neck and face, so when you wear the coat you sit very still, rubbing the fur against your cheeks. It is quite adorable! You are hands down the snuggliest little guy around. I'm glad you are small for your age because I can continue to hold you on the couch until you nod off for the occasional afternoon nap. When I pick you up you wrap your little arms around my neck and say, "I'm thinkin' about Mommy…" You are now in your big bed – but you prefer to sleep on the floor. You always gravitate to the carpet right next to your bathroom door. Sometimes Dad and I torment you by sliding our hands under the bathroom door to touch your head. You always respond by saying, "Goodnight…Goodbye." Anything to get us to leave you alone. You love to play, especially rough house! Hide and seek, chase, wrestling are all favorites. I enjoy watching you showcase your agility when you turn somersaults without using your hands and maneuver your way across the kitchen counter like a cat. You also enjoy the occasional game of chutes and ladders and Hi Ho Cheerio, but you definitely are a man of action when given the choice. You're a great eater – bananas, apples, grapes, mixed vegetables, water and always Cheerios! We just got you to enjoy chicken nuggets, fish sticks and hot dogs – we were certain that you would be a vegetarian up until just a few weeks ago. You are finishing your first full year of preschool at Cherry Tree (Jack's class was moved from Prairie Trace to Cherry Tree Elementary at the end of the 2005 school year) with Diane Knollman as your teacher. What a blessing she has been to our family. You were such a brave boy when the bus came for you the day after your third birthday. You cried on the way to school, but by the end of the week you walked to the bus all by yourself wearing your backpack. You are so quick to adapt and grasp new situations. Your language is showing consistent improvement and we are excited by your obvious delight in subjects like math, letters, and the solar system. You also know all of your letters and are learning the sounds each one makes.

By the summer of 2006, Jack was talking much more, though much of it consisted of lines from videos and talk that didn't match what was going on around him. For example, I might ask "What do you want to eat?" And Jack might reply, "Buzz-Saw Louie knows the true meaning of Christmas." Regardless of what he said, he was always very enthusiastic and animated in the delivery which made us smile. He was also playing better as far as using the toys as they were intended rather than just carrying them around. On one evening I heard him from the kitchen loudly humming in the living room. "Oh, God," I thought. "Here we go. He's probably sitting in the corner rocking back and forth." But when I went to investigate, he was running in circles flying his toy plane above his head as the engine "hummed." The next step would be for him to play with other children in a more give-and-take fashion. He was beginning to sit for longer periods of time for reading and taking part in back and forth conversations about the book. All exciting developments.

We took Jack to the fair when he was four years old and he *loved* it. In the evening Ed and I talked to him about it with him supplying two to three-word answers to our questions. We went back and forth with about five exchanges. We then realized that this had been our first true conversation with our son.

His second year of preschool brought more exciting gains in the area of speech as well as some truly humorous occurrences. One day he came home wearing different pants. Apparently, he had fallen into the toilet when he tried to sit on it. E-mails went between my husband and I to the effect of:

Dear Ed,

Your son fell into the shitter today at special ed preschool. Love, Mari

Dear Mari,

Thx for the update. Those harrowing toilet openings can be quite large for those with a 12-inch inseam. ox, Ed

Most people from Indiana remember the 2007 Super Bowl because The Colts won. I remember it because of the night Jack had. We had our friends, Doug and Sandy Delor, over to watch the game with their son, Drew, who was 5. I assumed that he would spend most of the evening playing with Betsy while Jack played alongside them. When Betsy and Drew went down to play in the basement, Jack followed, much to my surprise. We heard all kinds of laughter and happy shrieks from down below and then realized that Jack was also laughing. Whatever goodness was going on was being enjoyed by Jack too! This was a new thing.

When the game started, Betsy was all about watching the Colts win, but Drew and Jack chose to watch *Cinderella* in the den. I continued to hear all kinds of joyful sounds coming from the hall which made me smile ear to ear even as Chicago scored the first touchdown. Whenever Drew came out to check on the game, I would hear Jack yell, "Drew, come back!" Later, when Drew wanted to go to the basement again, I asked Betsy to go with him to keep him company. But Drew said, "No, I want Jack to come."

There were other breakthroughs. Jack was learning to read. He finally allowed us to use his alphabet blocks to spell out simple words. We had tried to do this with him many times and had been consistently rebuffed. In the past these blocks were only used to represent presents or anything else that is square. On a good day he would let us use them to build but that usually ended with him taking one of the blocks and just walking away. But this time he was able to sound them out and read them independently. (dog, cat, sit, pig, frog etc.) The best part was that he got joy out of it because we were all clapping and screaming. He wanted to spell more and more. It thrilled him to make us proud. He was also beginning to get his own paper and draw things himself and to write random words describing the picture. In the past, he always brought the paper to me and asked me to draw what he wanted. Now he was bringing us the papers to show us and to say, "Look what I made!"

Our birthday letter for his fifth birthday recalled not only learning achievements, but the fact that Jack was now playing with a neighborhood boy on occasion. Although this play rarely lasted long, it was so encouraging to see. I have such vivid memories from my own childhood of playing kick the can with the Hirschmans and flashlight tag at night. I recall the smell of the grass and how it always amazed me that it could become pitch dark without my taking note, because the degrees of change were so slight. Would he ever play with children like that and make such memories? Would kids ever come to *our* door seeking him out because they enjoyed his company?

1985 - My friends were everything to me. Would Jack ever have that?

April 10, 2007: You are now reading, counting past 100, and taking swimming lessons! You completed another year of preschool and are scoring above your age in reading and math. You have begun playing with Jacob, a little boy who lives two doors away. I love watching you chase each other with water guns, your small, wet, little bodies racing across the yard emitting shrieks of delight. You often add your sense of drama by running to the swing set and jumping onto a swing on your stomach as if to fly. And sometimes you run to the sand box and yell for help as if you have fallen into a pit of quicksand. It is all very dramatic! You also love going to the pool across the street. You look so sweet jumping off the step in your little life jacket or as you pretend fall into the hole of your blow-up ring. Or sometimes, you choose to "paint" the wrought iron fence a la Tom Sawyer. Regardless of your choice of activity it is always very dramatic and fraught with danger.

If uncertainty and fear were constants during Jack's preschool years, the person who helped us find our way was Diane Knollman. What I have always loved the most about Diane was her level of discernment and grace. On that grey day back in 2005 when I asked her if she thought Jack was on the spectrum she answered swiftly and with clarity. When my autopilot kicked in with "It's OK," she begged to differ. Not because she truly believed that God had dealt me a bum hand, but because she knew where I was in my journey. She knew that at that moment *it was not OK*. Diane also knew when tough love was in order. I once asked her if she thought Jack would be able to go to college. "How do you know Betsy will go?" She replied.

Touché.

Memories from the preschool years touch my soul in so many ways. To see an entire school administration *loving* my child and drawing him out simply floored me. I watched Jack's speech therapist walking him from office to office to help him become comfortable shaking hands and saying his name while maintaining eye contact. On picture day the photographer was about to do a retake on this one, but thankfully Diane said, "No way. That's Jack."

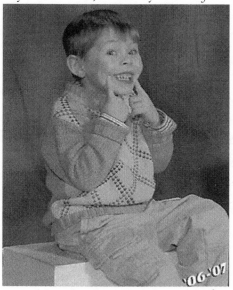

Jack's school picture from 2006.

Every IEP meeting left Ed and me shaking our heads in wonder at how well they understood Jack. When I visited the kindergarten room at Mohawk Trails Elementary to meet Jack's new teacher prior to his starting school there, I had to look away so she wouldn't see my tears as I pictured Jack sitting at his little desk in a sweater vest and jeans. Will he be able to have success in this class? Will the teachers love and understand him as they had at Cherry Tree? Will these neurotypical children sniff out his weakness and squash him like a bug? In years to come I would see God's hand in every transition Jack has gone through. He has always been faithful. But I was just starting my journey and my soul ached with fear. I wasn't the only one who found this transition bittersweet. Miss Ruth, Jack's bus driver had picked him up from our driveway for three years. She had

Saying goodbye to Miss Ruth, 2008.

The little bus leaving for the last time, 2008.

been struggling for weeks at the thought of not seeing his face in her rearview mirror any longer.

In the beginning I had been self-conscious about having the short bus pull up to my house. Now I found myself standing on the steps of it talking with Ruth at length about random things before she would pull away. When Jack was 5, he had invited her to come to Hilton Head Island with us on spring break -- along with several classmates, I later found out. When he got on the bus after our return he said, "Where were you? You didn't come!"

Ahead of us lay the great unknown of "real school." Could he do it? I was so frightened.

Arise – for this matter belongs unto thee. He will be with you. Be of good courage and do it.

Ezra 10:4

Chapter 12 – Glass Children

Before we talk about Jack's transition to kindergarten and mainstream school it is important to dedicate some time to his sister; Betsy, and the role she has played and continues to play in Jack's life.

Alicia Arena's TED talk describes "Glass children" as children who appear strong (note that they *appear* strong, not that they *are* strong.) Glass children are children who are growing up in a home with a sibling who takes up a disproportionate amount of parental energy; a sibling with an obvious physical or emotional disability, an addiction, a serious illness, or significant behavioral issues. The siblings of this child are called glass children because their overwhelmed parents look at them and rather than see their needs, look right through them.

We have a home movie from 2004 that kicks me in the gut every time I watch it. There are so many things going on in that footage that would not be detected by the casual viewer. It was during this time that I was first having serious concerns about Jack. I knew I was going to be taking the kids through the car wash and for some strange reason I felt compelled to take the video camera to record Jack's response. Betsy had loved the car wash at his age. She would squeal in delight and point to the pink and blue soap foam as it blew against her window. So, I aimed the camera squarely at Jack's face and waited. Hoped. Prayed for some type of response.

Nothing.

But that's only part of the reason this footage is poignant and heartbreaking.

In the background as I focus on Jack's face you can hear Betsy. I focus on him and wait, but it is her voice you hear. I tell her "just a minute" in the monotone of a person whose mind is elsewhere. But she implores me -- "Mom, look at me. Mom, take my picture. - Mom. Over heeeere! Mom! The dryers are there. *The dryers!*"

It's only in the last five seconds that I pan to capture her face. She is not angry. She is grace. She gives me a pass. Again. What must that have felt like to be ignored by me and how many times did she have that feeling throughout any given day?

In the movie, *Wonder,* with Julia Roberts, there is a voiceover by Via, the sister of a special needs child named Augie. It describes what it is like to have a brother with special needs. I wept in the theater when I first saw it. I cry every time I see it. Because it is her voice. It is Betsy. "Augie is the sun. And mom, dad, and I are the planets that orbit the sun. I love my brother and I'm used to the way his universe works. My mom says that on my fourth birthday I wished for a little brother. And when he was born it only took a few seconds before I was all over him. I've never asked my mom for help with my homework. Mom and dad would say that I am the most understanding girl in the world. I don't know about that. I just know that my family can't take one more thing."

Via is not bitter. She adores her brother Augie too.

As he prepares to go to middle school, she takes him by the shoulders and says, "If they stare let them stare. You can't blend in if you were born to stand out." There is a flashback scene of Via sitting on the beach at Coney Island with her grandmother, who tells Via that she is her favorite. Incredulous, Via asks, "But what about Augie?" To which her grandmother replies, "I love your brother. But he has a lot of angels looking after him. And you have me." She then takes a necklace from her neck and puts it on Via's. "You are everywhere. And you are my favorite."

We never spoke to Betsy about our concerns for Jack, but I distinctly remember the moment it become clear to me that she was all too aware. We were sitting at the kitchen table and she was working on her homework. I mentioned that Jack would soon be the same age as she was when we sent her to kindergarten. I believe I had been explaining to her why she was the youngest in her class – that we had put her on the bus just weeks after she turned five. I noticed that once this sunk in, she started to cry. She told me that she was scared for him. Afraid that he wouldn't be able to cope with "real school." I was taken aback not only by her discernment but also by her sincere care and concern for him. It touched me deeply. From our discussion, it was decided that Betsy and I would e-mail Mrs. Knollman and Betsy would be able to speak with her to discuss "how the grown-ups are going to get Jack ready for real school."

I never did hear from either Diane or Betsy the details of what they discussed. For a very brief period I was curious. But soon I realized that knowing the details would take away from the beauty of this tender mercy. Their conversation was sacred ground.

What happened at the program Diane put on for the parents to celebrate her class's graduation from Early Childhood provides vivid examples of both Jack's inability to decipher social cues and Betsy's steadfast devotion to him, her willingness to stand in the gap. Toward the end of the program, Diane read each child's name, and they walked up to the stage to receive a diploma of sorts. Most kids noticed the pattern – when your name was read you walked to the front. When Jack's name was called, he sat right where he was. He didn't even indicate that he had heard his name. Ed, Betsy and I were sitting in the back of the room.

After a brief pause and without any direction from us, Betsy walked to the front of the class, took Jack's hand, and walked him up to the podium. Afterward, she took him back to his place with the other kids and made her way back to us. She never looked at us or indicated that she felt

Jack graduating from Preschool, 2008.

she had done anything special.

As the summer of 2008 wound down, Jack prepared to attend "real school" at Mohawk Trails Elementary on bus 94 with his sister. He was reading, doing basic math and well-versed in colors and shapes. I was nervous about losing the support of Miss Diane. She was my eyes in her classroom and loved Jack as if he were her own. I prayed for the children in his class to be kind and patient with him. I continued to pray that he would catch up socially. It was very hard to accept the idea that Jack might always be a bit different than his classmates. That as he developed and made gains they would also mature, leaving an ever-present gap.

Simply put, I didn't know what to expect and it paralyzed me with fear. Would he be able to tell me about his day? Many times, he didn't want to talk about school, but I could get a glimpse of his day listening to him play. One day he admonished an imaginary friend that he "should not kiss friends at school" to which Jack replied in a different voice, "But these are my friends and I love them, and God made them special." I desperately wanted this little boy to know how special *he* was. This little one who "loved me to Target and back." There was a game that we played with regularity called "baby on the street." I would wrap Jack up in a blanket and carry him into this kitchen yelling, "Look, Daddy and Betsy! Look what I *found!?* A baby on the *street!*" That was Betsy's cue to implore Ed and me to keep the baby, all the while Jack would smile in satisfaction at our glee in finding *him*. These were such happy times.

Betsy was and is a tigress for Jack. She was so sensitive toward him it almost didn't seem fair that a child so young would carry such a fierce devotion. At one of Jack's Boy Scout events there were two boys playing catch. Jack left Betsy and me and went over to join the boys. When he asked for the ball to be thrown his way, they ignored him and started playing keep away, with Jack in the middle. Like a puppy he jumped up and down laughing as he tried to catch the ball. He didn't realize that they were making fun of him. Betsy, who was sitting next to me watching, lowered her face into her hands and cried. I quickly ushered her out into the hall where we both cried. As hard as it was to watch Jack being mistreated when he didn't even realize it, it was harder still to watch my daughter's heartbreak for him at the injustice of it all. I can't even recall what I said. What does one say at such a time?

Piglet: "How do you spell 'love'?"
Pooh: "You don't spell it. You feel it."

We have precious footage of Betsy watching out for Jack on his first day of kindergarten. As the big bus turns the corner, she puts a protective arm around him and utters words of encouragement in a voice that only he can hear. She told me that afternoon that Jack and the other kindergarteners had been instructed to sit in the front seats, so she was unable to sit with him as she had planned. However, she said, she watched the back of his head all the way to school and looked out the window to see him shepherded to the kindergarten rooms. During the two years they were in the same school, she thought about him throughout the day, hoping that he was doing well and not

Betsy and Jack heading to "real school," 2008.

Grandpa Jim and Grandma Kay wishing Jack luck at Kindergarten.

Mari Sandifer

becoming frustrated or scared. Fire drills were particularly upsetting for her because she knew how terrified Jack was of them. It must have been a lot for her to balance her day with concerns for her brother, whom she adored, and who was right down the hall.

At times Betsy was not only the "Jack whisperer" but also the "Mari whisperer." I recall a homework session that went south until both Jack and I were in tears. As if dropped straight from heaven to my kitchen Betsy swooped in and said something to the effect of, "I've got this." And she did. I left the room and she calmly took over. Who *are* you? I thought to myself. Yes, she came from me, but there is so much in her that comes from somewhere else. I never knew what the term "old soul" meant until I met Betsy. She has always instinctively known the best way to draw Jack out. She has always known that the goal was to get him to play interactively with other children. There is a video from 2007 that makes us laugh out loud as we watch an eight-year-old Betsy attempt to facilitate a game of tag between Jack and a neighborhood boy. At one point she literally runs into Jack and yells "*Tag*! I'm It!!" as if he'd tagged her. She then proceeds to physically push him and yell "*Run*!! I'm It!!" Watching her draw him out in video after video is magical.

Much of the bonding between Betsy and me throughout the years has been over Jack, and some of the situations we have found ourselves in are downright funny. Once, a neighborhood boy came over to swing with Jack. Betsy and I were curious about what they were discussing. I believe I have selective amnesia with regard to whose idea the next move was (because it's kind of creepy, in retrospect). The bottom line is that Betsy went down to say hello so that she could deposit her iPhone on the ground close by, in "record" mode. Yes. We bugged their conversation. Was that bad? We were relieved as we listened later. The conversation was only slightly strange, and the boy was extremely patient while listening to Jack discuss the specifics of pipe organs.

Jack doesn't like to talk about anything negative he might endure at school, but he sometimes feels comfortable sharing it with Betsy. One day he told her some things that were said to him by a tormentor. As I listened from the kitchen Betsy and I locked eyes and without a word we went all Cagney and Lacey, getting into my car and driving directly to this boy's house to confront him. On the way our talk crossed over into ten shades of ghetto that makes me laugh as I recall it. I believe something might have been said about how his mother will cry when she sees what we have done to him – and other non-Christian things. (I can't recall which one of us said it. My memory, you know…) *What fun to have this girl on my side*, I thought. Thankfully, the boy fessed up and hopefully learned an important lesson. His mother was wonderful about the whole thing, too.

Once when Betsy was away on a class trip, one of her friends stopped by just to hang out with Jack. Brooke took a selfie with him and offered to help him set up an Instagram account. I watched from across the room, humbled by the beauty of it. Surely Brooke's love for Jack was a result of the example Betsy had set for all of her friends.

It's strange to raise a child to adulthood. Today Betsy and Jack are practically grown, but in my mind, they are a mashup of themselves at every age. They only know me as "adult mom." I don't think any child can understand how powerful the mashup effect is until they have children of their own and experience this miracle. I have been there from the start. In 2016, Betsy had an experience of a lifetime when she played Belle in our church's production of *Beauty and the Beast*. More than ten thousand people came to the show, which was sold out night after night. During the curtain call I watched as Belle and The Beast came out. The spotlights created an ethereal halo effect over the top of their heads as the audience rose to their feet.

**Betsy and her friend, Jon Osgood, in
Beauty and The Beast, 2016.**

I saw that, yes. But at the same time, I was also seeing her cry as she told me she only got the understudy for *Annie*. That she did not get a call back for *Big*. That she did not make the choir she had wanted. I was seeing the first time she reached her arms out to me to lift her from the car seat and the times we were summoned by the nursery because she could not be consoled.

It was a joy to witness her receiving a standing ovation, especially from such a close vantage point. But what made it truly breathtaking was knowing the journey that had gotten her there. The journey that had gotten all of us there. You see, I know her backstory, and that is the richest part. Think of *Rudy*, *The Blind Side*, *Apollo 13*, *Soul Surfer*, *The Pursuit of Happiness* and *Miracle*. What makes us weep for joy when success becomes real? It's not the success alone, it's the success in light of the battle. The success in spite of the battle. The success that is a gracious gift because we don't deserve any of it. It is all just a glorious gift from our heavenly Father.

If I could give my children some advice for the future it would be this: The best and most compelling stories are rife with detours, peril, and internal conflict. Our most extraordinary heroes often have the deepest flaws. It's the yin and the yang. They strive with enthusiasm, and they fail with it too. If you are feeling overwhelmed by mistakes you have made in the past, please give them up to the Lord and aim yourself in the direction you are called. Learn from these mistakes, pray for forgiveness, commit to doing better and then *shake them off* and move forward. Jesus delights in redemption. Steer clear of people who want to keep reminding you of where you have fallen short in the past. Not everyone in your life is a good candidate for hearing your dreams and struggles. Don't waste your time trying to change their perception if they are set on seeing you in a certain light. Accept the fact that they have it wrong because they are, in fact, human. I get it wrong. They get it wrong. We are all doing our best. We are all just walking each other home. These are the thoughts that help me slay the nocturnal tigers. "Where would I be if I didn't serve a God who sweeps away our offenses like a cloud, our sins like the morning mist?" Reads Isaiah 44:22.

Mari Sandifer

For the last five years I have struggled with depression. This blackness has been like nothing I have ever experienced. I am still working through it. I fear that as Betsy has gotten older, I have put burdens on her that no child should have to endure. She has seen and heard things beyond her pay grade. At times I have felt like it was she who was raising me. Through it all she has spoken words of truth to me and shown compassion beyond her years. Because of this I fear that she dreads what her absence will mean for us who remain when she leaves for college. What I want for her more than anything is to know without a doubt that Jack, her father, and I will be okay when she leaves. It is not her responsibility to make sure we stay on the rails. I want to send her off like an arrow so that she can enjoy a season where the only person she needs to worry about is herself. To discover a life outside of our immediate family. To forge her own path knowing that she is utterly extraordinary. Irreplaceable. Beloved.

*You've developed the strength of a draft horse
while holding on to the delicacy of a daffodil.
You are the sister, advocate and protector of a
child with special needs.*

Lori Borgman

Chapter 13 – Elementary, My Dear Watson

lementary school went smoothly for the most part, and I have precious memories from that time. On weekends, Jack and I had a tradition of going up to my room in the evening to hang out on the bed and watch Everybody Loves Raymond. I would have my latest copy of *People* magazine and a large diet coke. We could hear Ed and Betsy playing games downstairs having the time of their life. They both loved games. Jack and I, not so much. I loved those times. We were safe. Jack was happy. We could communicate without words, and when Jack was young, he was a man of few words. We called him "Beaker" (Beaker is a lesser known Muppet character who says very little), but those words, as few and far between as they were, became all the more precious to me.

It was predictable and comfortable. Safe inside and away from the outside world I could adore him and connect with him in a way that no one else could. It was perfection to me. These were the nights I would lie beside him and watch his face, inches from mine, as he fell asleep. What a wondrous vision that was. It was also during these times that I recognized a kindred spirit in this little man.

One night as I changed the channel, I noticed a slat that was askew in the wooden blinds. I told myself to fix it, but then I forgot. About an hour later it caught my eye again and just as I was going to get up, Jack bolted from the bed and fixed it without saying a word. Those blinds were producing a shadow on the ceiling, a series of long dark lines of differing lengths side by side. I noticed his eyes studying it intently.

"What do you see, little man?" I asked.

"A pipe organ."

I studied his face, marveling at his imagination. His skin was translucent and alabaster. His eyes were like the blue of an aquamarine stone. They are still that color. And his lashes made me think of a giraffe's. One time while he was asleep, he smiled slightly. I asked him if he was having a good dream, not expecting that he would answer. But then he replied without opening his eyes, "I'm thinkin' about mommy." My heart.

The connection I feel to Jack is actually a gift. I believe God puts something special in the heart of a mother with a child who has special needs. It's an extra measure of boldness when it comes to that child. We are their advocate in a world that is predisposed to make fun of and ridicule those who are different. Because we have been there since the beginning our discernment is acute. We see circumstances that will cause our child distress when others see nothing. We see a change in the way our child is holding his body and know that he is suffering in some manner and trying desperately to hold it together. We see around corners and watch for landmines. We know what type of Nutri-Grain bar to buy and why nothing else will do. We know that asking for three oyster crackers and three saltine crackers at Steak and Shake is no laughing matter. When we act on this knowledge we are sometimes misunderstood. But if you are in that situation, please trust your instincts. Nobody knows your little one the way you do. There's no need to waste your energy being angry or trying to explain yourself. Some will not understand. Let it go. It's much easier.

Ed is an Eagle Scout and Jack became involved in scouting during first grade. I am so grateful that Ed took full ownership of this aspect of Jack's development. Anyone who has been through the program can appreciate the time it takes. Jack was at every meeting and campout. He didn't always want to go, but I am certain that this experience contributed mightily to his development.

Popcorn anyone? 2008.

Since I'm a fellow introvert, some of Jack's coping mechanisms delighted me. I recall pushing him in a shopping cart at O'Malia's supermarket one afternoon. We ran into Diane, the stepmother one of my best friends, Vicki (who I mentioned in the acknowledgements of this book.) Diane kneeled down in front of Jack and in a very animated fashion said, "Hi, JACK!" To which he put his hand out, turned his face to the side, and said "All done." So classic it makes me smile even now. Who hasn't wanted to do that at some point in their life? Thankfully, she was gracious and howled with laughter.

Regardless of his preference for being alone, there were exciting developments that reminded me of how miraculous the human brain is. Even if Jack wasn't neck and neck with his peers, he was still making social advances that thrilled us. Although he did not have play-dates with kids his age, he did begin describing certain classmates as his "friends." Michael and Maggie always brought a smile to his face when we asked about them, and I would often catch him staring at their images on his class picture. His kindergarten teacher, Mrs. Thompson, left mid-year to have a baby. I didn't realize how much he missed her until he asked if she was "done having her baby so she could come back." It warmed my heart that he had connected with her enough to feel her absence.

This is Jack, 2008. Fear him, 2016.

Jack also started taking Tae Kwon Do classes with Master Yoo. It wasn't his favorite thing, but he dutifully went twice a week for about six years. We could see great benefits for him in the areas of focus and discipline. He enjoyed getting a "check," a piece of colored electrical tape on his belt whenever he mastered a skill. In the beginning he used to cry if he didn't get one and it was quite pitiful. But with time he became brave and understood that "checks take time to earn." It took eight years, but Jack achieved the rank of black belt in 2016. I marveled during his ceremony. Again, seeing the "mashup" of Jack. My heart swelled.

Jack sharing his latest publication, 2010.

Jack enjoyed drawing, writing, coloring and cutting paper and often cracked us up with hilarious comic strips that often involved plays on words and harrowing experiences for the main character. Most themes involved a damsel in distress, explosives and flying body parts. I loved to listen to his play, which was always very animated. He didn't like to be disturbed, however, and if I tried to join in, I was often admonished. "No. I'm just talking to myself." He was so loving and precious. We developed a thing where we would look at each other from across the room and I would point to my eye, make a heart shape with both hands and point to Jack. Then he did the same to me but add "too" by holding up two fingers. I was very sick one winter and while I was resting, he lay down next to me and kissed my shoulder. Then he patted my back with his little hand and went downstairs to play. My eyes were shut the whole time and he must have thought I was asleep. That made it even more sweeet.

Jack rarely asked for anything. So, by God, when he expressed a desire for something, I did everything I could to get it for him. The first time he ever asked for anything, he was five years old and we were in Target. He saw a giant heart-shaped pillow covered in pink fur. He loved the feel of it and asked if he could take it home. I was so happy I could have cried. He could have asked me for a car, and I would have tried to get it for him. He carried it to the register himself, which delighted onlookers because it was literally as big as he was. I now sleep with that very pillow

Sleeping on his beloved heart pillow, 2007.

Mari Sandifer

every night.

The texture was what he loved about that pillow, and texture soon became a big part of our life together. I recall rubbing a satin pillow of my grandmother's when I was a child and noting how different it felt when rubbed at different angles. Children like Jack have very keen sensory issues and are calmed by certain textures and tactile stimulation, like how we are calmed by the sand on the beach. Jack still loves items that are soft and/or squishy, and he is a collector, so we soon began curating all things delightfully soft. Once in Hobby Lobby I told the kids they could each pick something for themselves. Jack chose a fabulous hot pink boa. At times like that I secretly thanked God for Betsy. In my mind she was his beard for such purchases. I would no longer care, but back then, for some reason, I liked that I had a little girl with me. Regardless, I was going to get Jack whatever grabbed his interest. He was finally making his wants and preferences known to me. It was my pleasure to honor them.

The funniest thing about this boa was where I saw it later that night. Jack was always fastidious about keeping his person and environment clean. Let's just say that when he needed to relieve himself, he often stripped down to his birthday suit to avoid the possibility of dipping a shirttail into the toilet water. After dinner, I walked upstairs and saw him sitting on the toilet. He was in the buff, except for the pink feather boa draped elegantly about his neck.

I learned that I needed to be on alert for those inner alarm bells that would tell me Jack needed something. Social situations wear me out and they do Jack as well. At gatherings of a large crowd I would often take him away from the action so that the two of us could spend time where others were not. This could mean ditching a cookout, sporting event, theater production etc. It always felt a bit naughty. We went for walks, acted out his favorite book, *The Carrot Seed*, and decompressed from the overstimulation.

The best was finding secret places that others didn't see like a room in the basement of an old house, a trail far away from the cookout, a crawlspace, a clearing through the trees that had a bridge. The goal was escaping, finding something cool that everyone else was missing, and enjoying it together. During that time, I was his favorite person to be with which I relished. I felt honored to be invited into his world. I didn't want to leave, and I resented anyone who tried to pull us out, to upset the beautiful equilibrium that we had.

When I didn't pay attention to my internal alarm bells, it was usually a mistake. For instance, an evening in the fall of 2008 didn't go well for our family. It was the Sunday after my nephew, Chris's wedding to Nattie in Bloomington. We had stayed at a hotel Friday and Saturday night, and attended the rehearsal dinner, the wedding, the reception, and the family breakfast. Sunday night, I should have stayed home with Jack, because both he and I were beyond fried. But it was Oktoberfest, an event we attended every year, and the kids loved it. We had also made plans to meet another family there.

I can't believe I was up for that given all we had already done that weekend. I was so much more ambitious back then than I am now. That particular year, Oktoberfest had moved from its usual location at picturesque German Park, where Jack had expected it to be. When we arrived, he was angst-ridden to find himself in a different place. Secondly, something about the acoustics there amplified the loud drone that all of the rides produced. It was deafening and relentless. Jack covered his ears and hummed loudly. I was also affected by it, but I just thought I was in a really shitty mood because I was tired. No question. My whole brain was foggy from the din and fatigue. I followed Jack and worried about him. Betsy followed me. It was difficult to communicate because we couldn't hear each other for all of the noise.

Ed and I were sideways with each other that night because we were tired and had been snapping at each other in the car. So, we were not working as a team. Somehow or other, the kids and I got separated from Ed and the other family. We had no iPhones, and I had no money. It was bedlam. When we did find them, I was in the doghouse. Everyone thought I had just walked away with the kids. That wasn't at all what happened, but I couldn't explain it to Ed and our friends, and nobody believed me. It sucked. All I knew was that I had to get Jack comfortable because he was in utter distress. And Ed and I needed to spend the evening in different locations lest we venture deeper onto the set of Jerry Springer.

I saw up ahead of us a row of bounce houses. I knew the kids would love that, and there was no time limit on that area; they could bounce as long as they wanted. Most kids like to bounce, and many kids on the spectrum love it. It helps them feel grounded in their body. I took Betsy and Jack there. Ed would spend the evening with our friends and join us at the end when it was time to go.

But when I got to the entrance, I was shocked at the

number of tickets required to get both kids in. I didn't know if I could drag the kids all the way back to the ticket booth and then back to the bounce houses. I remember looking at the man saying I didn't have enough tickets. I have no idea what he saw in my eyes, but he took the tickets I had in my hand and motioned us in. *God bless him.*

Betsy and Jack ran off to bounce and I sunk into a lawn chair close by. The next two hours were utter bliss. I didn't have to talk to anyone and could just sit and watch them having the time of their lives. The noise didn't assault Jack's ears while he was bouncing, and he and Betsy acted out dramatic falling scenes from various Disney movies. All was well with the world: Jack was okay, and I was in a chair by myself not disappointing anyone. But I was very much alone. When you're alone with your thoughts it can be hard to sort out what is true and what is a lie. The devil loves that.

I wish I had listened to my inner voice that night. The one that would have said to Ed, "No way am I taking him to Oktoberfest after the weekend we have had. That is courting disaster. You and Betsy go and have a wonderful time and we will be here waiting when you get back." But back then I wanted to appear unflappable. Strong. Game. I wish I had known then that there are other ways to be strong, like knowing your limits. In the end the wheels fell off and that evening cast a pall over the whole weekend. I wish I had been braver and advocated for myself as strongly as I advocated for Jack.

Chapter 14 – Turduckenesque

Second Presbyterian Church, Indianapolis, IN, 2013.

As a parent of children on the spectrum we are always trying to find things that are good for *our child*. Not things that are good for children in general. We live in Carmel, Indiana – where sports are a big thing for little boys and girls alike. I was never into sports. It's not in my genetic makeup. Nor is it in Jack's. In the early years that troubled me. But as time went on, I grew to love the way we spent our time together. The wedding we had attended on the "ill-fated Oktoberfest weekend debacle" had been held in a glorious church that housed a breathtaking pipe organ. That was how Jack discovered this instrument, and it was love at first sight. We started using Sundays to visit churches around Carmel and Indianapolis that had pipe organs. I would sit in the pew of the church watching him take it all in and smiling to myself, thankful that I wasn't outside in the hot sun watching a soccer game.

A few years later our family made a trip to Bloomington for Indiana University's homecoming. Our first stop was at the First Presbyterian church to visit the pipe organ that started it all. In the car Jack mentioned that he had been praying he would get to play a pipe organ on this trip. (*yikes.*)

First Presbyterian Church, Bloomington, Indiana, 2014.

I always tried to allow Jack as much time as he needed during these excursions. On this day Betsy and Ed were antsy to get to the next location. I suggested that they go ahead, and we would meet up with them later. Jack and I stayed longer at the church and then went to Alumni Hall to see a recently installed pipe organ there. To our delight someone was on the balcony behind a curtain playing it as we arrived. After each song Jack clapped with enthusiasm. It was so sweet. After a few songs I saw the curtain being pulled back. Apparently, the organist had heard the applause and his curiosity was piqued. When he saw Jack and realized that it was only the two of us, he invited us to come upstairs. "*So that Jack could have a chance to play it.*" I marveled at this turn of events. I doubt we would have received that invitation if it had been all four of us. I can vividly recall bringing up the rear as the three of us climbed a set of stairs. A single tear ran down each of my cheeks as I watched Jack, knowing that his prayers had been answered.

Admiring the Alumni Hall pipe organ at Indiana University, 2014.

We ended up making many trips to Bloomington just to visit the pipe organ, so we came to know the staff at First Presbyterian Church. They were extremely gracious to Jack and allowed him to play their organ on occasion. Jack took to sending emails to Chris Young, the man who plays this beautiful instrument for the church. Here is one of them:

Dear Chris Young,

Thank you so much for letting us visit on the summer of 2014 to see the Austin electro-pneumatic opus 2407 pipe organ at First Presbyterian Church in Bloomington. I think you are a great organist of the church, especially during Chris and Nattie's wedding. When you played Handel's Air from Water Music, Bist du Bei Mir, Canon In D, The Trumpet Voluntary, The Lord's Prayer, The Trumpet Tune and Widor's Toccata. It was beautiful. I love the console, the pipe display, the cloth screen, the wooden barrier and everything about the organ.

Sincerely,

Jack Sandifer

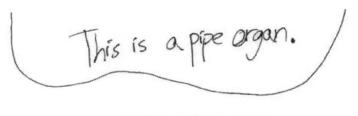

A Jack Original

Mari Sandifer

I am always thrilled to be able to get something for Jack that I know he will enjoy because he rarely asks for anything. As his interest in pipe organs grew, I started finding faux organs throughout the house that he had crafted using various sticklike objects--(Lincoln logs, bats, the wand attachment from Ed's dry vac...) I started trolling eBay for used pipe organ pipes and happened upon several available for pick up in Chicago. A three-hour drive felt like nothing compared to the bounty of pipes I was about to acquire.

When I arrived, I explained to the seller that Jack was on the autism spectrum and had a passion for this instrument. He paused for a moment and then brought me to another room. He had built a miniature pipe organ with twenty-five pipes. A real working pipe organ on a miniature scale. The idea of getting this for Jack left my plan for buying random pipes in the dust. I will never forget that Christmas and the joy on his face when he saw it for the first time. He couldn't BELIEVE that it truly worked like a real pipe organ with a wind chest and fan. He loved taking each pipe out and blowing through it to hear the different tones. Such a treasure!

In the fall of 2017, First Presbyterian replaced the original pipe organ that had been Jack's first love. I asked if I could produce a time-lapse video of the installation of the new organ to thank them for their hospitality over the years. I was delighted when they offered me some pipes from the old organ to give to Jack as part of his Christmas. I smiled to myself as I caught a glimpse of my shadow in the parking lot toting an eight-foot-tall pipe horizontally to my rented U-Haul. This was not a scenario I would have envisioned for myself by any stretch. God is funny that way. Those pipes are propped up in the corner of our basement and I smile every time I see them.

Do you love theme parks? Crowded water parks? I don't. The noise, the smells, the heat, and all the rest make me want to jump out of my skin. Jack is also bothered by these things and he developed a coping mechanism that I found intriguing.

I'll call it "Jackhum." I've noted before that Jack often hummed when excited. He also hums if there is a noise, song, or person that assaults his senses, Jack hums loudly to drown them out. (Like a white noise machine from Sharper Image.) But Jackhum 1.0 was glitchy. The sound stopped when Jack paused to take a breath. This issue was addressed in Jackhum 2.0, where Jack makes a loud gasping noise when taking in air, thus keeping the noise going continually. Jackhum 2.0 is still in beta but works well enough for Jack to use it on occasion. Full release is TBD.

When Jack was young, we went to the supermarket every Saturday. They often hired people with disabilities to bag the groceries. There was one bagger who had autism. He was by far my favorite bagger because of his attention to detail, but he had a habit of peppering me non-stop with questions, never pausing to allow an answer.

"Do you like *Hannah Montana*?" "Do you like *The Suite Life*?" "The Colts won on Sunday." "Do you like football?"

On one particularly harried day as I left the supermarket, he offered to help load my groceries in the car. All through the parking lot he fired off questions in rapid succession. Apparently, Jack was not into it, because he started humming. Loudly. Hearing each of them on either side of me made me literally laugh out loud at the absurdity. And at God's sense of humor.

Jack's autism continued to present me with more unexpected experiences. Such as going to the parking lot where all the Carmel Clay school buses reside. Jack loved school buses. He liked how they were parked in order by number, the differences in their shapes and grills, and counting the number of windows in each. Back then, the buses were unlocked so we also played hide-and-seek. Betsy came too! Jack spent *a lot* of time thinking about the bus numbers and the number of windows each bus had. This proved tricky when we were driving because if we happened upon a bus, he insisted on knowing the bus's number and how many windows it had. And because I enjoy the way my eardrums allow me to hear, I made every effort to slow down or speed up accordingly so that Betsy and I would be able to get this information for him *stat*. But alas, sometimes I couldn't make it happen.

On one such occasion, when Jack asked for the required information, I told him I had not been able to see it. *Wrong. Freaking. Answer.* I looked in the rear-view mirror at Betsy in horror as Jack began wailing and speaking in tongues, Betsy yelled, "94! It was bus 94! And it had 18 windows."

Jack was immediately silent. "*Oh my God*," I thought, "*she just pulled those numbers out of her ass.*" I glanced at her in the rear-view mirror and she returned my look with one that was that was two parts "Seriously, must I do everything?" and one part "Aren't you glad I am here?" I was both proud and horrified at the same time.

Where the BUSES LIVE!!!

By the way, did you know that buses have emotions?

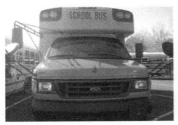 

This bus is happy.

This bus is angry.

It was 2009. Even though I had been making great strides in the acceptance department I still worried way too much about how Jack appeared to those on the outside looking in. For instance, when he thought something was exceptionally funny, he took to galloping around the room or down the street, humming loudly. Around this time, he also started taking a shine to Betsy's princess dresses. I thought he looked darling. Those pastel confections were all over his color wheel. Ed didn't like it, but any honest American dad will agree that they would rather not see little Billy dressed like Ariel. Who can explain it? We live in a fallen world. Lastly, Jack had no interest in learning to ride a two-wheeler. He was perfectly fine leaving his training wheels on. None of these things gave me pause. When taken individually.

What *did* give me pause was the possibility of these three events intersecting in a perfect storm. A turduckenesque trifecta of social missteps from which he would never fully recover. The vision of seeing my seven-year-old son humming loudly to himself while riding a training-wheel-equipped bicycle and dressed like Snow White was too much to bear. I spent much time on high alert, watching Jack to make sure he didn't do anything that would bring ridicule. It was exhausting and futile. In time I simply gave up and decided to enjoy my son.

I continued to marvel at how my life had turned out. I was doing things I had never dreamed I'd be doing. And I was thoroughly enjoying it. I often found myself in situations thinking, "This is not anything I would have ever imagined myself doing. Ever." And then I'd laugh at God's sense of humor. It was true. I was finally making my way toward peace with Jack's situation. What a blessed relief.

He will once again fill your mouth with laughter and your lips with shouts of joy.

Job 8:21

Chapter 15 – The Essence of Jack

Some children on the spectrum can have trouble interpreting facial expressions and even noticing when they have changed. That's why they often miss social cues and continue to "talk it up" on a subject long after the listener has displayed obvious boredom with it. Learning all these social and interpersonal nuances separately and on purpose is a huge challenge. I was talking with Jack one night and changed my expression slightly as he spoke. He paused, studied me, and then asked, "What does that face mean?"

His question displayed such an earnest desire to get it right that I had to look away for a minute. With our kids we need to remind ourselves that they don't mean to appear rude in their actions. If they seem clueless in a social situation it is only because they haven't learned yet how to handle that particular situation.

One day Betsy had a friend over and when her mother came to the front door to pick her up, I was in the kitchen and Jack answered the door. She told him she was there to retrieve - we'll call her "little Susie." I heard Jack say, "Okay." Then silence. For thirty seconds. I walked out to see what was going on. The woman was just standing at the door looking slightly confused. Apparently, after she made her intention known, Jack said okay and just walked away. He knew to answer the door but not what to do after.

That's where these special people are often misunderstood. Jack does not look unusual to anyone. Some forms of autism do not present themselves physically in one's appearance. When our kids miss it, they are often met with harsh and incredulous stares. If no one is there to advocate for them or to explain to them what happened for future reference, they are left feeling like a failure and unable to figure out how to prevent it from happening again. I know that many people on the spectrum have no desire to learn these nuances and don't understand if they act insensitive or hurt someone's feelings. Their insensitivity should not be taken personally, however. I'm very lucky that Jack is crushed when he commits a gaffe and tries earnestly to get it right the next time. Knowing that Jack wanted to learn and could retain information we set about teaching him social scenarios. One at a time. Before you give me too much credit let me just say that there were many times I saw an opportunity and said to myself, "Screw it. I wonder if Betsy's home, so we can watch *Sex and the City?*"

I have found that when I take the time to ask Jack why he does something a certain way it's more than just missing a social nuance. He sometimes sees circumstances in a different way. When this occurs, I am reminded of how intricate and magnificent the human brain is. Many times, I thought I had prepared him well for a situation only to find that I had missed a very important and obvious piece.

If you are female and over the age of forty-five you remember the movie *Ice Castles*. Robby Benson's competitive-figure-skating girlfriend has become legally blind quite suddenly, though she can still see shadows. Rather than bow out of the upcoming competition they decide she will skate without telling anyone. She skates beautifully but falls when taking the victory "cry and wave" lap. Why? Because they had not planned for the flowers on the ice!

Here's one of Jack's *Ice Castle* stories. When we planned to go to Disney World, we told Jack that we would be taking lots of pictures in front of things so that we could remember the trip and show others what we had seen. I noticed that lately he was doing a very interesting pose with his left arm in each picture. Jack liked to over-deliver, so he rarely just smiled for a photo back then. He always brought that something extra. Call it "flair" if you will. I couldn't get him to tell me why he was doing this pose whenever a picture was taken. Nor could I get him to stop. So, I let it go. The trip was hectic and overstimulating for Jack and me. Are we speaking truth? I HATE DISNEYWORLD. The only thing I hated worse was knowing how much we had spent to be there. I'm so sorry. I know it's like saying I hate babies. I don't. I LOVE little babies!! But Disney was on Betsy and my husband's bucket list. A MUST.

So much flair...

...So little Time.

So back to Disney. Not literally (thank God). I saw Jack over at a replica of a Star Wars vehicle. I looked away for a minute, and then back in that direction. I saw a family who had decided to take a photo in front of the vehicle, and there was Jack. Posing *with* the family. The parents were confused and looking around for assistance. Not only was he posing with them, he was proudly bringing the flair. He felt very secure in his position next to grandma (someone else's) and was very angry with me when I pulled him out of the lineup. "Why can't I be in the picture!? I'm a cute kid!" he wailed.

This was a scenario I had not remotely considered. Who knew that while teaching him about taking vacation photos I should also clarify that one should not interject their person into *other people's* vacation photos? Back then I recall feeling sad about this. If I were the person then that I am now, I would have laughed very hard. I might have even waited a beat or two before intervening…just to watch. But this was new, and I had no idea how Jack's story would end. If he was missing such things now, how was he going to survive as an adult? How could I possibly prepare him for every time he misses it? And how will he be treated at school when things like this happen? My God, what will become of him?"

It wasn't always gloom and doom, though. We had some hysterical moments when coaching Jack as a family in preparation for an event. We actually practiced opening birthday presents before his family party, because at Christmas Jack had been very clear when disappointed by a gift. We acted out the wrong way to behave, exaggerating greatly, which made him laugh. Then we gave him faux bad gifts so he could practice being thankful for *everything* (underwear, a pencil, toilet paper). It was hilarious to watch him say, "Thank you. That is so nice." in a robotic voice. During his party we all kept looking at each other as he opened presents trying not to laugh. By the time of the party his enthusiasm was less robotic and more sincere. However, at one point he almost went rogue and Betsy yelled, "Turn off the camera!" (Ed was taping the festivities), but Jack recovered quickly. We were very proud.

This was a very special time for our family because we were seeing encouraging things and felt that we could "exhale" a bit. And even laugh. At times Jack can be more articulate than an average child his age because he has had so much speech therapy. He is a poster child for early intervention! This can be quite humorous at times. Ed and Betsy love to play games, and even though Jack usually doesn't choose to join in, they always ask him. Once when he was only eleven, he walked past the table where they were setting up Apples to Apples. They asked if he would like to play. At first, he simply answered, "No," as he walked by. But then he stopped, backed up and said, "But thank you for asking. It looks like a lot of fun." There was also the time that he texted me while I was grocery shopping to request apples. The text that followed requested green apples and apologized (with complete sincerity) if that made him a racist. Jack is substantially above average in some areas, but shockingly below in others. It's almost like his brain is so busy thinking about the things he loves that he misses things that are obvious to average kids.

I remember coming to pick him up from his Sunday school class in 2008. I used to arrive a bit early so that I could spy on him from the hall, which could make or break my day, depending on what I saw. I was still telling myself, "If he is acting normal that means everything will be okay." What I defined as "normal" and "okay" back then is still up in the air, but I continued to torment myself with these games, like an emotional cutter. One Sunday I smiled to myself as I watched him run his glue stick across the back edge of the Jesus he had cut out and then carefully turn the paper over to press it into place. "God love him," I thought. "Maybe he will be a pastor. An autistic pastor for Christ…"

"Wait. Why is he turning it back over?" He rubbed more glue stick on the back. Then he paused and tapped the end of the glue stick with his little finger. Then he SMELLED the glue stick.

Then it hit me. "Oh my God, Jack!" I thought to myself, "Take the cap off. The cap is *on* the glue stick. That's why it's not *working*, Baby!" But he didn't receive my telepathic message and there was no one there to help him. He didn't get upset. He just kept trying to rub glue onto the back of his flat Jesus. He was six years old.

When Jack was younger, he was a bit of a loose cannon. He doesn't slap himself in anger like he did at five. But for many years we lived on high alert, especially in public. Parents of kids on the spectrum, and their siblings, form mental lists in their head of situations and activities that will not end well. These things are to be avoided at all costs. To outsiders this looks like enabling or coddling, but to the family of a child who is on the autism spectrum it is a matter of survival.

Here is an example, in the form of a play (because I am active in community theater and wanted to be an actress when I was growing up):

Jack: *(shows picture to person)* I drew a bus.
Person: That is a great drawing!
Jack: How many windows does it have?
Mari hears what is about to happen from upstairs and starts running to intervene. Betsy, who is in the kitchen, also hears, drops the fork in her hand and runs toward the family room. Dad is at the grill but can't get in because he accidentally pulled the French door shut and is now locked out.
Person: Let me count them. one, two, three…, fourteen. It has fourteen windows.
Mari: Jesus, Joseph and Mary. We are *too late!*
Jack: NOOOOOO! (Guttural sounds, self-slapping and supine thrashing ensue.)
Betsy: *(to person)* Oh my God – you included the

driver's side window in the total, didn't you!?

Mari: *(to person)* Judas Priest! How could you have done that?! The driver's side window NEVER factors into the total, and God help you if you think it does...Now get the h*ll out of my house!

(I don't really say that last part, but that is what I am thinking.)

I remember how he loved to stand on the window ledge with me behind him to watch Betsy during her swimming lessons. He hated when I took him down at the end. It got to the point where I would apologize to the room beforehand because they were about to get an earful. He did not disappoint.

Jack tends to worry at times, and his concerns can spiral out of control. One thing he was very concerned about as a child was storms. He hated storms. The lightning flashes and claps of thunder sent him over the edge. When he was a toddler, we used to find him in his closet with the light

Birthday party/Family Tornado drill. There's a special place in heaven for these folks.

Mari Sandifer

on to disguise the lightning outside. It was a workaround he came up with on his own and I thought it was brilliant. But what he *really* liked to do before a storm was to talk about it. To worry about it. To estimate if a tornado would, in fact, touch down. It was never-ending. In fact, at one family gathering Jack had the entire family do a mock tornado drill.

His concern could be grating, so one night we all lost our patience and told him he was only allowed to ask if there was going to be a tornado once every fifteen minutes. I believe we even set the timer. We looked forward to fourteen minutes of peace after each inquiry. But as the night wore on, Jack began to get desperate. And creative. At one point, after only six minutes of the fifteen-minute cycle he said, "It's a good thing we are not going to have a tornado...*right*??"

Jack knows that he misses things and sometimes how this knowledge manifests itself makes me sad. He has no interest in having an Instagram or Facebook account. Most parents would be thrilled, but when I asked him why, he said he was afraid he would "make a mistake" or "do something wrong" online. Even after I offered to check his posts before he made them, he did not want to venture down that path. So, I imagine he is still concerned about his social interaction. It must be hard to be uncertain in this way, and I feel bad about that.

He does like to view Facebook using my account. He loves looking at pictures of people he knows from school. Even though none of them come to our house or socialize with him, he considers them his friends. My mother recalls that I never wanted to play with kids after school either, but my teacher reassured her that I did play with kids at school and that perhaps after being "on" for six hours I was exhausted once I got home.

While we try to teach our children all about life, our children teach us what life is all about.

Angela Schwindt

Chapter 16 – The Tigers Come at Night

There are certain memories that when conjured up between the hours of 1:00 and 5:00 in the morning virtually guarantee I'll get no more sleep. These are the recollections of times when I lost my patience with Jack or forced him to act "normal" out of pride, with no regard for his spirit or his mind. In a blog post, Shannon Rosa explained that because we live in a society that "fears autism and disability… parents believe their autistic children must be forced to act and feel like non-autistic people, even when their children are obviously miserable."

My own failures have been epic.

I pushed my autistic child's head under water. On purpose. Many autistic children are ultra-sensitive to smells, noises, textures, overstimulation and other experiences that others find bearable. Their brains are just wired differently. But these differences aren't apparent to strangers, so when these kids can't tolerate the assault on their senses or miss a social cue, they are often seen as misbehaving or being contrary or stupid. The kids are left feeling like they have done something wrong, but they don't really know what. Who can blame them for wanting to be by themselves? I would too if I couldn't figure out the rules to a game that I didn't even want to play.

When Jack was five, I must have still been in denial, or perhaps I had taken one too many Tylenol PMs when

I decided it would be a good idea to sign Jack up for swimming lessons with three of my friends and their typically developing children. The lessons were held in an antiquated indoor pool that reeked of mildew and echoed like the inside of a drum. We'll call the teacher Bev. I can't remember her name, but if I could I would likely want to change it for this story. Bev did not cotton to little boys who screamed and wouldn't follow directions.

The smell, the noise, the uncertainty, and fear wreaked havoc on Jack's brain. Now fold in a dose of tough love from Bev and I would say I had positioned myself for a real shitshow. I saw Jack stiffen up when Bev tried to work with him. It was the pitiful rigidity of a tiny boy sensing that he was not safe or loved by this woman. I can still see his shiny little fifth percentile body.

On this particular day I was ultra-sensitive to the differences I was seeing in Jack. I was scared. And jealous of my friends, whose little ones jumped into the water with delight and played on the stairs of the pool while waiting for their turn with Bev. I wasn't talking to anyone about my fears then. I was hypersensitive any time Jack responded strangely to a situation and hypersensitive to other people's reaction to Jack. I watched for glances between women and hushed conversations that stopped when I entered the room. In a word, I was full of pride and paranoia. It was so terrible. I watched their children interact and play together while Jack hummed to himself.

I recall feeling smug taking Betsy to playdates. Once she got over that whole projectile vomiting thing, she was a real delight. She talked circles around every child and sang show tunes. I didn't realize how much her behavior stoked my ego until I had a little one who didn't knock it out of the park socially at every turn. I knew it was wrong and that just made me feel worse. I was angry with myself for wanting Jack to act differently. I knew that it took him a while to warm up to others and I knew that Bev didn't have the patience. I could not watch him go rigid in her arms and look at me with those pleading eyes. I was the person who kept him safe. I was the one he wanted because he trusted me. So, I insisted on holding Jack myself.

Oh, how I betrayed him that day.

Everything had gone wrong. I was tired. He was scared and wouldn't put his face in the water. I watched all of the other kids doing it and I thought, *Man, once he discovers this "underwater world" he will LOVE it! We won't be able to get him to the surface!* It's true. At seventeen Jack goes to the neighborhood pool at least once a day in the summer. But he wasn't seventeen that day. He was five. And in frustration I angrily told him to put his face in the water.

He looked at me in confusion. Why was I mad? I could see the wheels in his head turning. But I said it again. "Put your *face* in the *water*!" He started to cry and said, "No." So I did something that still makes me sick to think of. I shoved his face into the water. On purpose. The look he had on his face when he came up is forever seared into my brain. His eyes were wide open, and he held his mouth as if forming the letter "*o*." He was in shock. And the nauseating way I tried to play it off sickens me to this day. "See Jack! Wasn't that fun? You are *so brave*!" As if he had a choice. He was so shocked he didn't even cry. And then it happened. For the first time since his birth, I felt him go rigid in *my* arms. Unsure of what he had done to make me do that, he became afraid to move lest he cause me to do it again.

He was totally at my mercy. He didn't trust himself or me. Can you imagine how helpless he must have felt? Kids on the spectrum don't pick up on things that average kids learn through osmosis. If I had done that to Betsy, she would have boxed my ears and deafened every dog within a five-mile-radius with her screams. But now I know that Jack was trying to figure out what he had done to cause me to betray him. His precious brain was coping with so much already and now I had added to it.

I have apologized to him many times over the years about it. Finally, a few years back, he told me I could stop telling him I was sorry - that I was a good mom. Or maybe he just didn't like thinking about it because it made him sad, too. What I would give to do that day over.

I set my son up for rejection. There was a boy who lived on our street who was Jack's age and one day he was playing in his yard with three other little boys. For some ungodly reason I suggested that Jack go out and play with them. The boys were sweet and had tried to play with Jack before. But it never lasted for more than fifteen minutes. It would start out rich with promise. Ed, Betsy, and I would run to the window to watch excitedly. There would be the usual back and forth and maybe a ball would be thrown. Once. Then Jack would start to look at the house. He would say something (or not) and then just walk away and come inside leaving them to scratch their heads while we yelled "No!" at the window and watched helplessly. So, after a while they stopped coming to the door. Who could blame them? But it made me sad. Betsy had friends over all the time. The girls played with Jack and he *loved* it! And they sincerely enjoyed playing with him. I didn't take into consideration how Betsy facilitated interactions between Jack and others so seamlessly that one stopped thinking she was a factor. Until she wasn't.

Some days I just refused to accept reality and it seems laughable now-- but talk about sending him to the wolves. That day I shoved Jack out the door and told him to go "play with the boys." He hesitated, and I could see the wheels turning. He didn't want to go. But he did want to please me. So off he went. I stood in the screened-in porch to listen. It was painfully awkward. I could sense that the boys didn't want him there. My precious Jack. My favorite person in the world. The dearest soul. Then I heard one of them say, "Let's go inside." There was a pause and then I heard the declaration that shattered my heart. "Not you."

It got worse. Jack didn't understand. He said, "But THEY are going---" referring to the other boys who were walking up the stairs. "But you are not invited," one of them said. The thought that they would not want him around never entered his mind. I ran out of the porch and called him to come.

"Jack! Let's watch a movie and make popcorn," I yelled, my heart sinking. I wanted to make a quick pivot with a promise of *VeggieTales* and popcorn, the same way I had tried to smooth over the incident in the pool with "You're so *brave!*" I watched him slowly walk toward me and I hoped beyond hope that he would not be able to understand he had just been rejected.

But he did understand. As he walked toward me, he was crying. Then I was crying. And so was Betsy, who had seen it too. He sat on the red ottoman in our family room and said, "Why couldn't I go in? I'm a good kid." Seeing him hurt killed me. *How many times does this happen at school?* I asked myself. Does he have anyone to play with at recess or eat with at lunch? What must he think of himself if people are telling him they don't want him? That he's *not invited*!? Does he recall rejection as he lies in bed at night waiting to fall asleep? Does he ever cry in bed after we kiss him good night because he dreads having to go to school the next day? I stood in the kitchen looking out the window at the little shitheads, who were now playing outside again. I hated them. I hated them for not recognizing the gift of my child. I hated a world that was so confusing in its nuances. I hated that we lived in Carmel, an upscale community where children seemed kissed by the gods of academia, athletics, and artistic pursuits. I hated myself for pushing him out there. I hated that I wanted him to belong. I hated the world because I loved my son. And I knew the world would not be kind to him. I had hoped that it would, but we were not there yet. The "everybody counts" and zero tolerance on bullying were giant leaps forward, but not enough for Jack. How could I possibly be there to help explain things to him at every turn? It was heartbreaking to watch him trying to make sense of the world and all of its nuances. I felt heartsick that I had caused the interaction.

Because Jesus loves me, He sent Betsy in at just the right moment and spoke to me through her, as He often does. I didn't look away from the window, but I could see her approaching me through my peripheral vision. I felt her hand rest on my back. "It's okay, Mom. That's more Jack for us." She was nine.

Mari Sandifer

*I think with any sort of rejection, you're sad
that you weren't enough for that person.*

Jennie Garth

Some "tiger" memories, however, aren't the result of my action, but someone else's. I recall taking Jack for a check-up before he was going to the third grade. As we exited through the waiting room Jack saw a "friend" from school. He was sitting alone without a parent. "Hi, Bill!" Jack said. No response. Just an icy stare. "Bill, are you sick?" No response. *"Are you kidding me?"* I thought. I stared the kid down as if to say, "Cat got your tongue?!", but he was not the least bit intimidated by me or my icy gaze. I took Jack's hand and got the heck out of there. "Well, Bill wasn't very talkative today, was he?" Jack asked. He was so innocent and still is. He had no idea Bill* was ignoring him on purpose. Who knows? He might ask Bill to be one of his groomsmen because they are such good friends.

name has been changed to protect the asshole.

It was bad enough watching him struggle to understand what comes naturally to so many. To think that I had ever added to his confusion or discomfort with my own self-centered actions is difficult to get past. Even after all these years.

There is a woman whom I admire very much, although we have never met. Her name is Amy Wright and she was the 2017 recipient of CNN's Hero of The Year Award. She is a strong Christian and has two children with Down syndrome. I went to high school with her husband, Ben. I was moved to tears as I watched her acceptance speech. She spoke to her children and said, "Bitty and Beau, I wouldn't change you for the world. But I *will* change the world for you."

Amy, thank you for those beautiful words. You are releasing untold numbers of parents from the shame of feeling sad that they are going to have a child with learning or physical differences. It's not that they wish their precious child were different. The sadness comes from wanting the world to be different, more patient and accepting of all people. The sadness comes from the depth of love they have for their special child, the tenderness they have in their heart. It's a joke between Betsy and me that Jack is our favorite person. We sometimes compete for his attention. I believe it's because we want to build up such a wellspring of love and acceptance in his heart that when the inevitable happens, he will think to himself, "No. That's not true. I am not weird. I am extraordinary. Because my parents and my sister tell me I am every day."

So that has been our workaround. If we couldn't always be there to look around corners, we would fill his ears with words of love and encouragement. My sadness was not because I wanted Jack to be cured of autism. I adore every autistic thing about him. He is uncommon and exceptional. My sadness was because I knew he would be misunderstood and hurt because we live in a fallen world and kids can be cruel. I didn't have this figured out back then, so I spent many years feeling shame because I was sad. Thank you, Amy Wright, for setting the masses free with your life-giving words.

Mari Sandifer

The moment a child is born, a mother is born as well.

When you have brought up kids, there are memories you store directly in your tear ducts.

Robert Brault

Chapter 17 – Thanks for your sperm. Now please die.

This chapter is not fun to write. I'll say that right now. But putting this book out without sharing these truths is not an option. My hope is that you will find encouragement. It's hard knowing you have made mistakes and thinking you are the only one who struggles. It isolates you and gives credence to the condemning voices in your head. It makes the bad things easier to believe. We are born for community. Sharing not only helps others avoid common traps, it helps those who have also fallen short to step out of their shame. To be able to say, "You too? I thought I was the only one."

Even as we felt hope regarding Jack's future, Ed and I were struggling. All parents clash over decisions made rearing children. When a child has disabilities, the tensions can run high. The differences in temperament between two spouses are often magnified when there is a child with challenges. There is a grieving period that goes with coming to terms with this new reality. It will be experienced and acted upon differently by each person, and special attention must be paid to understanding your spouse and respecting their point of view. I made so many mistakes in this regard. In retrospect, I am thankful that I married someone who sees things differently than I. As I look back over the years from a higher level, I see now what Ed brings to the table as well as my contributions. They are very different, but complementary. But in the thick of things, it was easier to fester and act out in fear than to acknowledge the good that Ed brought. For many years we did not act as a team. And it almost ruined us.

Have you ever done that thing where you are lying in bed and your spouse is extra late getting home? Your mind starts to drift and to think "I wonder if he has been in an accident? I wonder if he is dead? I wonder how long it will take the police to get here?" Then you go further in the scenario and start to plan which black St. John knit you will wear to the funeral, how you will spend the insurance money, when you will start dating again.... Only to be pulled back to reality by the sound the garage door opening.

"Shit. He's still alive."

I confessed this fantasy to our marriage counselor and she told me that it is *very common* and didn't indicate that I truly wished him dead. This was a relief.

For parents of little ones on the spectrum, the marriage failure rate is about 80%. There was a point in our marriage that my husband and I came very close to divorcing. It is, in my mind, a miracle that we are still together, and it is truly by the grace of God. This chapter will not be a "she said – she said" freakshow. I am simply going to share some stories that illustrate *my* culpability in the struggles we have overcome and are overcoming as I write. There are two sides to every story, and the side I share will be the times I fell short. Just me. My hope is that if readers are doing or have done any of the same things, they will see that they are not alone. That there is someone else whose soul is as black as theirs. In addition, that they will stop.

I read once that when people get married in their twenties, they often choose partners who are their opposite in many regards. When people get married after the age of forty, they often pick partners who are more like them in temperament. Ed and I fall into the first group - we were both twenty-six. Common sense would say that teaming up with someone who is very different from yourself would be a positive thing. That these complementary outlooks would be a great foundation for a family. On a good day we recognize this. When we are both healthy and at our best the alchemy is beautiful. But as years become decades life has a way of kicking the shit out of you. I was so pompous in the beginning. I looked down my nose at people who got divorced. Surely any problems could be overcome with counseling and prayer.

Then I got married. Things happened that gutted us. We became more and more adept at pushing buttons. We stopped respecting each other and the things we brought to the table. On good days I recognize this, but after a sleepless night I enter my day with major "lizard brain." Ready for a fight. Ready to misinterpret things to the point of paranoia.

There is a certain dance in marriage where partners adjust their behavior to balance that of their spouse. That has always seemed to be our pattern. If one goes to one extreme, the other goes the other way, with equal intensity. If everyone is operating at their best this can be beautiful. A symphony created by two people with complimentary gifts. But when life's stressors push everyone to their limits these differences can be maddening.

Passive Aggressive Much?

Ah yes. Passive aggressive behavior was and can be my weapon of choice. It's cool because if anyone calls you out on it you can quickly turn it back on them because your actions will not have been overtly rude. And if you really want to be an ass you can then be righteously indignant that they even suggested that you said or did something with malicious intent. This will serve two purposes:

- It will make them begin to question themselves.

- They will think twice before confronting you again because they will start to doubt their own feelings. Cool, huh? Not really. It's actually pretty shitty. And also, not a great example for your kids.

In case you aren't clear on what being passive aggressive is, here is what the Urban Dictionary says:

Formerly associated with a particular psychological disorder stemming from years of perceived underappreciation and **bitterness**. A character flaw brought on by a person's inability to deal with their own bitterness, anger, or resentment in an **assertive** manner, thus, becoming a more passive form of hostility. See also: petty, little bitch.

Oh, the examples I could share. In the interest of time I will only unpack a few. Here are some of the more epic in outline form, for clarity purposes and in case you are taking notes.

I. Whitewashing the entire exterior of our brick home. While Ed was out of the country. Yes, it did look better, but I also knew that he never would have agreed to it if he had been asked. It was disrespectful of me and a terrible example for my children.

II. Hijacking the roll of "good cop" at every turn. This comes back to the balance phenomenon mentioned earlier. Whenever Ed needed to express anger it was a given that I would *not* support him but would automatically go to the defense of the children or whoever he was angry with. This made him look like the hot head and me the patient Zen lady. As time went on it changed the whole dynamic of our marriage. It became one of taking sides. Of not having each other's back. My opinions also lost all credibility because why would anyone take them seriously if they were *always* the opposite of yours?

III. Acting like a third child – One of my specialties was doing fun things with the kids that I knew Ed wouldn't have approved of because they are dangerous, against the rules, expensive etc. This was where "good cop meets fun playmate." The kids knew that dad would not approve, which cast him in the role of "wet blanket."

Examples include but are not limited to:

A. Taking a blow-up kiddie pool to the large pool in our neighborhood at midnight and getting into it (with Ed's MacBook, pillows and a down comforter) to watch *The Devil Wears Prada* as we floated along.

Why not good?

- No one is supposed to be in the pool past

10:00 pm.

- MacBooks don't respond well to pool water, nor does bedding.

- The kids knew Ed wouldn't go for it, so this set a terrible example on how to treat one's spouse.

B. Building an indoor sledding hill with every pillow in the house and sledding down it while standing up.

Why not good?

- Great way to break a collar bone, rupture a spleen, etc.

C. Bringing an extension ladder into the house so we can be on the ledge over the front door watching Netflix on the laptop while Ed was at work.

Why not good?

- Great way to break a collar bone, rupture a spleen, etc.

D. Taking the kids out of Betsy's window to sit on the roof of the screened in porch.

Why not good?

- Great way to break a collar bone, rupture a spleen, etc.

E. Overspending, with a twist – I have saved the best for last. I'm not good at everything by a long shot. But I am really good at making things look pretty, and when we were in the early stages of our journey, I used spending as a coping mechanism.

I still do it, although on a much smaller scale. But it is definitely something I am STILL working on.

If my mind was a scary and uncertain place, making my surroundings as perfect and beautiful as possible became an obsession. Hardwood floors, silk window treatments, new light fixtures etc. I reveled in the compliments I received at every Christmas party about how great the house looked. And of course, there was the endless trickle of used Chanel and Burberry jackets from eBay that kept the dopamine flowing. It's amazing how I rationalized the sheer volume by the fact that they were "used."

What is the twist, you ask? The twist is that I also got credit cards in my name, that Ed didn't know about. That, my friends, is called financial infidelity. Here's how Wikipedia defines it:

> When one spouse is making significant financial moves without the knowledge of the other, it endangers the financial future of both people and exhibits a disregard for the most fundamental parts of a healthy marriage: trust and communication. Financial infidelity can simply wreck a marriage when it is uncovered.

The rationalizations I used were as laughable as they were plentiful. "I make good money…I can pay for these things…they are in my name not his…I'm spending money on things for the house, not for gambling on the horses or scoring blow…he was a jerk to me today so screw him. I'm going to buy this _____ (fill in the blank)"

I have to wonder how I could have thought that I could live that way with no ramifications. Even if I never got caught, how did I think I could possibly stomach the fact that I had acted in this manner? I didn't recognize myself. The fear and sadness I was dealing with were now colored by shame and disgust in myself. Life loses its luster when you can't look at yourself in the mirror.

Please hear me: *nothing* you can touch or get compliments on is worth that feeling. To this day I struggle with using shopping and decorating as therapy. I am certain it comes down to pride. When a person is insecure the opinion of others becomes all-important. I felt that I was falling short in so many areas. I worked feverishly to buff the outside in order to look successful. All the while my soul was becoming an empty shell. My mind a swirl of dark thoughts.

I will never forget having to come clean with Ed and tell him everything. It was brutal. But so necessary. I like to say that Jesus loves me too much to allow me to stay where I am. In this particular situation there was much evidence of His grace and faithfulness, since I was forced to live through the repercussions of what I had done. The main miracle was that Ed did not leave me. Living with the secret of having excessive consumer debt is like acid for your soul. Especially when you know that others think you have it all together. I most certainly did not. I have and MBA in finance. I knew better. But I will say that looking the demon in the face and asking it to dance will set you free. If you are doing any of these things, please stop.

If you have already done this and are living in the shadows, tell someone. Anyone. Let your mistakes be known. Owning them fully is the only way to get free from the shame and fear. I also believe that the depression I have been struggling with for the last five years was brought on by not living authentically. Your soul can only take that for so long. Being in a career that I hated and knowing that I was overspending made me feel like a fraud. Nothing is worse than knowing that people would be disappointed in you if they knew the truth. And nothing is better than coming clean and finding that those who matter most love you anyway.

I wonder how it must feel for Ed to be married to me? I have been told that I act like one of those horses before the gate is opened, thrashing to get somewhere, to learn something, to produce something, to have mattered to this world. I try many things. More than the average person, I think. And I fail more too. Yet I can't stop. There are projects that I can't not do. It must be hard to live with someone like that. Someone who goes ninety-five miles per hour with her hair on fire and then crashes for two days. It must be frightening because lately I specialize in unpredictability. I am nothing like I was at twenty-six. This actually makes me very happy, but it must be incredibly frustrating for Ed, who thrives on stability and routine. He probably feels like he has had four - five wives in the last twenty-five years. But he has just been one husband. Tried and true. Steady Eddie.

Beyond being passive aggressive, through the years there have been times when I purposefully gravitated away from Ed and drew closer to the children as a way to escape his (perceived) judgement. Little children are incredibly gracious. Jack thought I hung the moon. You have heard the saying "I wish I was half the person my dog thinks I am." Given that Jack needed extra help, and that he thought I was the bomb, hanging out with him was a very attractive option. It could even look noble on my part, to be dedicating myself so much to him. But the bottom line is that this behavior created distance between Ed and me, which is not a good thing for any marriage.

Any home that revolves around the children will become a house of cards because our goal should be to produce independent adults who have their own lives. Having a "children first" dynamic results in a home of empty nesters who have nothing in common. I believe strongly in marriage counseling. Even if you feel solid, having a safe place where things can be discussed with an objective party can be invaluable. And striking while the iron is cold will pay enormous dividends.

I find that there is a pattern to the way my brain feeds me incorrect information and I am amazed at how often I can make the same mistakes. When I am doing well in my business, feeling competent and strong, I will believe the lie - that I can do all of this alone. And better. Thankfully, it never fails that a season of feeling this way is followed by a gut-wrenching course correction. An eye-opening bitch slap that brings me to my knees. Only then am I reminded that I would be lost without my husband. I would be lost without Ed. Our entire family would be.

When I think of every way I have failed my family and Ed, it always seems to circle back to the sin of pride. Pride says, "I don't want anyone to know I am struggling, because then they will think I am weak." So, we stay in our head. We live in the shadows. And we get off track by degrees until we look in the mirror and not only do we not recognize ourselves, we don't want to recognize ourselves.

Mari Sandifer

It is difficult seeing disappointment in the eyes of someone you love. At a certain point it hurts too much and the easiest and safest thing to do is avoid them. Then there is the lie "I just need to bail and start fresh with someone who doesn't have all of this dirt on me." But really, it's not the shame that Ed is putting on me that is the problem. It's the shame I am putting on myself. And that is one massive-ass steam trunk I would haul to any new relationship no matter how shiny and new.

The most difficult thing in the world to do when we are feeling down on ourselves is to admit how we feel. Again, it's pride. Yet, self-disclosure is what we need to do to stop the cycle of shame and blame that so many of us get caught up with. Telling someone you have made a mistake and asking for forgiveness feels counterintuitive. We're afraid that if we admit our faults, we'll feel even more ashamed. But the opposite is true. The more we're able to say, "Yes, I messed up," or, "Yes, I made a mistake," or, "Yes, I'm sorry for what I said," the better we feel about ourselves.

There is something to be said for a marriage of twenty-five years that produced two amazing children. You don't chuck something like that aside without first analyzing every nuance of your own behavior. Because really that is the only thing I can control. Myself. Instead of wanting to get away from a person because they know about the ugly in me, perhaps I should lean in and recognize the miracle that they have stayed *despite* the ugly in me.

When we first met, I was an accountant. I stayed in that job for seventeen years. But it wasn't me. It was me wanting to be perceived as a person who reads The Wall Street

Journal, when in reality; I read People magazine. Ed is the most stable person I know. Even as a child he was called, "steady Eddie." He has held his current job for seventeen years, and I can't imagine him ever leaving it. Ninety-five percent of the drama in our home has been caused by my career transition, my overspending, my depression, my shortcomings. Many by now would have said, "I did not sign up for this." But Ed has remained.

My absolute favorite part in The Greatest Showman is the end when PT Barnum runs home and then to the beach to find his wife. When he said, "I've brought hardship on you and on our family. You warned me. I wouldn't listen. I just... I wanted to be more than I was." I looked at Ed and said, "That is me." Could my depression be caused by shame from past mistakes? The fact that my daughter is about to leave for college? The reality that starting your own business is *terrifying*? Hormonal because I'm Fifty? I'm sure it is a combination of all these things. But I recently started doing a new thing. And I think it is going to help. I have come out of the shadows. I am talking to people about it. I am writing this book. Do you want to know how to get past the fear that others will find out about your weakness and mistakes? Go ahead and tell them. It will take the wind right out of the devil's sail.

When parents first learn that their child is on the spectrum, there are many difficult emotions to process. There is a very real period of mourning that cannot be avoided. It is a sadness for the life you thought you would have and the realization that it is going to be different. There is fear. The spectrum is large, and there is a waiting period before you know exactly what you are dealing with.

When these challenges struck our family, we did circle the wagons, but then we drew our guns in fear. And aimed them at each other. We lost sight of the distinctly beautiful and equally complementary things that each of us brings to the family. We tore each other down with looks and actions. We lashed out with words we wish we could now take back. Some of the things my children heard us say to each other would make your blood run cold. So there is that. And with that comes gut-wrenching regret. Because these events will be remembered as a part of Betsy's and Jack's childhoods. I recall during our marriage ceremony there was a part that said our home would be a place of peace. Never in my life did I anticipate the ugliness that I was capable of. But it's no surprise to God. And he delights in bringing redemption to the direst of circumstances. His favorite thing is pulling us from the mire inch by inch. So that we can get back to the work of living in a way that honors Him.

See—I am doing a new thing! Now it springs up; do you not perceive it? I am making a way in the wilderness and streams in the wasteland.

Isaiah 43:19

How can I ever find peace in light of all of the ways that I have fallen short? One of my best traits is a steely determination. The dark side of this trait is what compels me to try to "make it better" with a dogged pursuit that runs ahead of God. But the bottom line is that some things just can't be "made right." Some things just need to be put in the past and learned from. It's only after we show grace to ourselves that we can begin enjoying the life that God has for us. It is never too late. There is never a point of no return as long as I continue to seek Him. Life through my brain, which is often on fire, can be exhausting. The touch of madness that causes me to spin is also my greatest

January 22, 1994

Fall 2018

gift. It fuels my creativity and enthusiasm. The following passage in Cheryl Strayed's book *Wild* touched me deeply.

"What if I forgave myself? I thought. What if I forgave myself even though I'd done something I shouldn't have? What if I was a liar and a cheat and there was no excuse for what I'd done other than because it was what I wanted and needed to do? What if I was sorry, but if I could go back in time, I wouldn't do anything differently than I had done? What if yes was the right answer instead of no? What if what made me do all those things everyone thought I shouldn't have done was what also got me here? What if I was never redeemed? What if I already was?"

His love roared more loudly than her demons.

~anonymous

Mari Sandifer

Chapter 18 – The Middle School Years

Sometimes it feels like Jack is in the no-man's-land of the disabled. Jack was ready to leave Mohawk Trails and venture to Clay Middle School. As Betsy and I took him to register, practice opening his locker, and walking to his classes several times, we saw a sign for "Best Buddies." If your child had disabilities, you could request a Best Buddy for them. This person would make sure they had someone to eat with at lunch and perhaps go to a football game or two with them. I looked at the sign for a minute and looked at Betsy (then fifteen). I didn't have to say a word. She read my mind and summed the situation up accurately and succinctly. "He's not disabled enough to get one, and he's too disabled to be one." Ya. She just said a mouthful.

Betsy helping Jack open his locker, 2015.

It was during these years that Jack became involved in music and community theater. His first show was The Music Man, in which his sister also played. Many other shows followed at Clay Middle School and our church, Grace. Since I also have the bug, there have been some shows that featured all three of us. The beauty of those memories will be forever etched into my mind.

Jack in The Music Man, 2011.

Jack adapted to having his classes take place in different rooms and started to make the high honor roll. There was a point in Jack's Middle School education that he tested out of being on the spectrum. This had always been part of the fantasy I had for Jack. That day they would look at me and say, "Well done, Mari. You *cured* him!" and the ticker-tape parade would begin, and bounce houses would be inflated. We would all live happily after. And the day was *here*! "Yes – please take it off of his IEP!" I said with great certainty. He was going to the high school soon, so now he could go there with a clean slate, like having a rap sheet expunged.

Mari Sandifer

Within three minutes, his counselor said something that completely shifted my paradigm and caused me to tell them to leave that ASD label right where it was. "They don't know Jack yet," his counselor said. She meant that if they didn't see ASD on his IEP a level of grace will have been removed. Until they got to know him better, they would misunderstand him and perhaps break his spirit with their responses to him. The thought of Jack being in a new environment where he wasn't loved (yet) made me want to make sure they knew at a glance that Jack was on the spectrum. It was his safety net. Like bumpers at the bowling alley. I think it is very important for people to be educated on the behaviors that indicate a person might be on the spectrum and I believe we are headed in the right direction. Public awareness has never been so high. But wouldn't it also be fantastic if people also acknowledged the flip side? What makes these people so remarkable?

Templin Grandin was born on August 29, 1947; in Boston, Massachusetts. She was diagnosed with autism as a child and went on to pursue work in psychology and animal science. She has become a leading advocate for autistic communities and has also written books and provided consultation on the humane treatment of animals. In addition, she has taken strong positions on autism and the education of children with autism. She advocates early intervention, including the training of teachers to direct each child's specific interests. She is a champion of neurodiversity and argues that her contributions to the field of animal welfare would not have been possible without the insights and sensitivities that are a consequence of her autism.

Mari Sandifer

There is a glorious TED Talk by Faith Jegede "What I've Learned from My Autistic Brother." I couldn't begin to do it justice by paraphrasing it, so here is a quote:

> "My brother is twenty-two years old and non-verbal, but he conveys joy in a way that some of the best people cannot. He knows what love is. He shares it unconditionally. He is not greedy. He does not see skin color; He is incapable of lying. He reminds us of how little we know about the human brain and how wonderful the unknown must be. Doesn't he seem incredible? But most people don't agree. Because his mind doesn't fit into what society says is normal. He is often bypassed and misunderstood. But what lifts my heart is that even though this is the case, although he is not seen as ordinary, this can only mean one thing: that he is extraordinary."

Rosie King is a young woman with autism who has also shared a powerful TED talk. In it she describes how she has thousands of secret worlds going on in her head at the same time. For Rosie there is the "real world" and then there is the world in her mind, which is often much more real than what is happening in reality. The beauty, for her, is that she has no desire to fit into a perfect box doing the things that are expected. In her talk she explains that the joy in her head gives her so much energy that she must find an outlet for it which can result in running and/or screaming.

What was cute for a toddler is not for an adult woman, but Rosie is pragmatic. She says that her unusual behavior separates the wheat from the chaff, leaving her with friends who are genuine and true. She has two siblings who are more highly affected by autism and considers them the most amazing people in the world.

If we can't get inside the person's mind no matter if they are autistic or not - instead of punishing anything that strays from normal, why not celebrate uniqueness and cheer every time someone unleashes their imagination?

Rosie King

I wrote the following letter to Jack on his thirteenth birthday that truly summed up my feelings at that time

April 10, 2015 - What an exciting year you have had. You just finished the sixth grade at Clay Middle school, and any fears we had about your leaving Mohawk Trails were soon put to rest. You always seem to rise to the occasion. I recall being told by someone when you were three that you would always perform at a "below average" level. This year you were on the high honor roll. So, to that person I would like to respectfully say:

Bite. Me.

It appears that you officially inherited the theater gene, just like your sister. This year you played the understudy role for Michael Darling in Peter Pan at your school. What a pleasure it was to see you up there, fearlessly executing your lines and enjoying every minute of it. I sat in the audience and marveled at what I was witnessing. To think that there was a time when we didn't know if you would speak. When I see you now and recall the journey that got us here, I am filled with awe and gratitude.

I am afraid I struggled this year with a feeling of sadness and a sense of foreboding that I could not seem to shake or explain. There was an afternoon not long ago that I was standing at the kitchen sink looking out the window. I was crying about something that I could not quite put my finger on. I could see you approaching in my peripheral vision and you stood quietly next to me. Without saying a word, you simply patted the tears on my cheeks dry with your bare hands. It was as if God himself were touching me. Then you said something that I will never forget:

"You're doing a good job."

I laughed to myself because I immediately thought. "Why Jack Sandifer, I do believe that you have made 'Theory of Mind' your bitch."

This year we took a trip to Michigan with extended family. I watched you reading a book to your cousin, Will, and was proud of how loving you were to him. The way you continuously strive to "get it right" in a world that can be so confusing inspires me. I know it can be frustrating, but please be patient with yourself when you do get it wrong. It's your response that says so much more about the man you are becoming. There is a genuine desire to learn and you seem to bring that trait to every situation. We went to Indiana University's homecoming last fall. You were thrilled to visit the pipe organ at First Presbyterian as well at the new one at Alumni Hall. It was such a treat to watch you look up at them and smile, capturing numerous photos with your iPhone. You brought your yearbook with you and at times your gaze would alternate from the pipe organ to certain photographs as you smiled broadly. You said you were pretending that your friends were here enjoying it with you.

That made me sad – I know how much you enjoy sharing the things you love with others. I asked if it made you sad that they weren't here, and you said "no" in a way that left no doubt as to your sincerity. Again, I realized that if you say you are happy, I need to take that at face value. When you were a toddler, I craved for you to show me things. I wanted so badly to be taken into your world. Now I fear that there are times when I act impatient if a YouTube video you want me to watch feels too long. When you ask me to watch a movie with you there are times that I peck at my laptop even as I know you are wanting my full attention on the movie. Your joy is watching me laugh at what you find funny. As we lock eyes and laugh at the same things there is a powerful connection that I fear I take for granted. I am so sorry for that. You and I have had many excellent adventures together. Betsy was in a play in Anderson this year and the two of us spent countless hours hanging out in the theater as she rehearsed. I simply cannot believe that I lived thirty-four years without you and didn't even know what I was missing. I recall sitting across from you and Betsy one night at Bob Evans restaurant. I marveled as I thought "There is no other place on earth I would rather be than with these two remarkable people."

As always, I love watching you and your sister. You have taken to sleeping on the floor of her room on Wednesday nights. You remove her desk chair and sleep with your head under her desk as if in a cave. You are moving right along in Boy Scouts and Tae Kwan Do. I know these things are not your passion, but I am proud of you for your perseverance. I am thankful that dad pushes you at times when my inclination would be to leave you alone. He really is doing you such a favor because we are at our best when we are being stretched. I look forward to seeing what you bring to the future. I am thrilled that you enjoy theater. You truly have a talent and seem to have virtually no inclination for stage fright. Like your sister, you bring it every time. I am proud of you. I am proud of your heart.

Jack dancing at his cousin, Hollyn, and Alex's wedding, 2013.

Mari Sandifer

This is a FOREVER journey with a creative, funny, highly intelligent, impulsive, strong-willed, loving individual. The nurse said to me after six hours with him "He is a gift." INDEED, he is.

Janet Frenchette, Parent

Chapter 19 – Carmel High School

A s I type these words Jack is a going to be a Junior, at Carmel High School this fall. How can it be that the little boy I used to scoop up with one arm is now seven inches taller than me? His voice is deep now. He has hair on his legs like a man…

Mari and Jack, 2018.

For anyone who is doing the math, Betsy left us for college in the fall of 2018. For kids like Jack, the anticipation of such an event is often a hundred times worse than the event itself. But I will say in this particular case, it was not pretty.

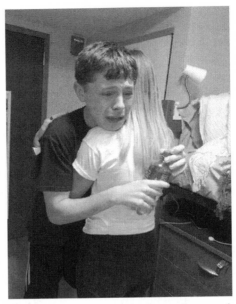

How lucky I am to have something that makes saying goodbye so hard, 2019.

Winnie The Pooh

But kids like Jack rally fast. By that evening he was completely over the fact that she was gone. But not in a bad way. Just in a matter of fact way. I consider it as blessing. She visits often, and he also goes to stay with her for weekend visits.

Sometimes, when I am low on sleep and it is 3:00 am, I fear for Jack. He has such a big heart. We liken him to Will Ferrell's character in the movie, Elf. So earnest. So gentle. Will he get his heart broken and will I be able to bear witnessing that? Does he want children? Will he have them? And if not, will he look longingly at families and be lonely at night? I used to think that he always wanted to be alone – but anything to the extreme becomes old.

I have been out a lot lately, working. Last night I prepared to watch a movie in the family room where Jack was, but then considered going downstairs where the TV is larger and the setting cozier and hermit-like. As an introvert I had had my fill of people and craved solitude. When Jack asked me where I was going it struck me as a distinct possibility that he would prefer that I stay. He confirmed as much when I asked him. Then, because he is so dear, he apologized for having this preference, because he knew that I wanted to go downstairs. I told him how happy it made me that he wanted my company. That seemed enough for him, so he went back to looking at his YouTube videos. He didn't want to talk, or even watch the movie I was watching. It was the presence of a warm body. Or was it me? I hope it was that he wanted *my* presence. Just to know that I was sitting there in case he wanted to ask a question or show me something. I felt honored and happy that he wasn't completely anti-social.

I have asked Jack before if it makes him sad that he isn't invited to social events and doesn't go anywhere on the weekend. He said absolutely not, and that seeing people during the school day is enough for him. Again, I circle back to the fact that he is genuinely happy. One thing that absolutely delighted him was seeing people from his early childhood class who are now at Carmel High School. Many of these kids had attended different elementary and middle schools so he hadn't seen them in ten years. I couldn't believe how much time had passed since we were waiting in the front yard for the little bus. I listened when people told me it would go fast, and I tried hard every day to take it all in. But still, I feel like it slipped away in the blink of an eye.

After Betsy's First Ball State Production, 2019.

"If Ever there is a tomorrow when we're not together... There is something you must always remember. You are braver than you believe, stronger than you seem, and smarter than you think. But the most important thing is, even if we are apart... I'll always be with you."

Winnie The Pooh

Mari Sandifer

Sometimes, when I allow myself to go there, I picture Jack as a thirty-five-year-old man alone in his house wishing for someone to want his company. He might very well be happily married with six kids at thirty-five, but in my weakened state, my mind goes dark. I felt this loneliness in my early twenties when I couldn't seem to make a man want my company. Going through that loneliness yourself is one thing. But imagining your child going through it is devastating. The phrase "I can taste the salt in your tears" comes to mind. For parents, we can also put that salt in our eye and in the open wound of our heart when our offspring suffer. And when that offspring lacks certain tools to cope - tools that were so freely given to everyone else, it is almost unbearable.

But then I realize that I have felt this feeling before. When I visualized him going to "real school," when wondering what lunch would be like for him? Recess? And middle school…high school…dropping him off alone at the homecoming dance that he had told me about just days before. He was wearing a bow tie, khaki pants and a sport coat. I watched him walk away from the car all by himself toward the school and I tried to picture him as a small boy. But I could not do it. I could not look away from that man he has become.

I recently read a very cool article about Amy Schumer, the comedian, and how she is married to a man on the spectrum. (She is also pregnant with their first child.) Here are a few compelling quotes from this article:

> "She told the audience about a time when she fell while she and Fischer were taking a walk, and instead of asking if she was OK, he "froze." "I

remember laying on the ground looking up at him, and I wasn't mad. I just thought 'huh,'" Schumer said. "Lot of 'huh' moments." Schumer said her husband's blunt honesty makes him a "dream man."

"Once he was diagnosed, it dawned on me how funny it was because all of the characteristics that make it clear that he's on the spectrum are all of the reasons I fell madly in love with him," Schumer said.

When asked on Twitter if she is concerned that her future child might be on the spectrum, Her response was priceless,

"How I would cope? I don't see being on the spectrum as a negative thing. My husband is my favorite person I've ever met. He's kind, hilarious, interesting and talented and I admire him. Am I supposed to hope my son isn't like that?"

I knew I liked her!

It's so quiet here without Betsy. Not only is she more talkative and louder as a person, she often comes as a package deal, with a few friends in tow. Jack is Jack. Quiet, except for the occasional humming, laughing, or singing. I love when I hear him singing upstairs in the shower. I always secretly wished that the movie of my life would include the moment when we discovered his savant skill, and that it would be him singing like Josh Groban. Out of nowhere would come the voice that would launch a thousand tears. The special skill. What is the part of me that keeps wanting that moment? If I'm honest with myself it's that I want him to get the attention that he craves. The attention that his sister got as Belle at our church. The standing ovation. The Susan Boyle moment. I want that for Jack.

Or do I want it for me? Is it still the pride machine in there wanting to produce something that really delivers? The kids that add so much to the world? Because then, by the transitive property, it could truly be said of me that I added so much to the world. But perhaps I need to be a bit kinder to myself. Is it pride, or simply wanting to matter? To be remembered? To inspire others somehow. Who didn't identify with Susan Boyle, and whose soul didn't cheer when that audience went from laughter, to awe, to ebullition – as if to say "We are sorry. We stand corrected."

Last week we got some glorious news with regard to Jack's long-held desire to sing a solo in a choir concert at the high school. You have to understand Carmel High School. There is something in the water in these parts that produces offspring with off the chart athletic, academic and artistic abilities. Think "Glee" talent. I have fantasized about selling the zygotes of married Carmel couples in their late twenties-early thirties as a cottage industry. Me and mine would be set. Betsy is currently in the musical theater program at Ball State University, which has a very low acceptance rate. She never made the top choir at Carmel High School and didn't receive a callback for a musical play until she was a junior. In a word: brutal. So, Ed and I prayed together on the morning Jack left for the bus to find out if he got his solo. We knew choir was first period and I told him to text me. I never heard anything all day and was not home when the bus dropped him off. I texted to see how his day was but didn't press when he responded. "Fine."

Dreams are the seeds of change. Nothing ever grows without a seed, and nothing ever changes without a dream.

Then I got home. The screaming and jumping were intense as he reported that he had been chosen for an eleven-word solo. "This counts, mom. Because I get to walk up and sing into a microphone." God bless Baby Jesus, Mary, Joseph, John the Baptist, and that whore who broke the perfume bottle! But truly, God bless his choral director, Katie Kouns, for her creativity in allowing three boys to have their Susan Boyle moment. Because anyone who has had a conversation with Jack in the past two years has been made aware, at length, of his desire to do this and his faith that "God will make it happen because he has been praying for it and God has a plan for his life and God put the desire in his heart so it must come true." I love to watch people's faces when he says those words. I can see the wheel turning. "How to respond. How to respond. Oh, God, how to respond…"

He is in the kitchen right now talking to himself. When he does this but doesn't want us to know what he is saying he disguises his voice and it sounds a bit like the adults in

Charlie Brown. I love his work arounds. He still hums too at times, but it's a bit disconcerting now that his voice has changed. Sounds a little creepy, like the dude from Sling Blade.

He recently finished his Eagle Scout project and was addressing envelopes to thank those who had donated their time to help. My heart sank when I saw that he had swapped the locations of the receiver address and the return address on the envelopes. He would have to start over and do them all again. This sort of setback is torturous for him because he is task-oriented and thought he was done, but also because he was a bit embarrassed. I felt for him again when I saw him licking the corrected envelope to close it knowing that they were the type of envelopes that you don't lick, but rather, you pull off the strip to expose the sticky flap. It gave me a flashback to when he tried to use the glue stick without taking the cap off. He never noticed they weren't sticking until I brought it to his attention. Again, he was embarrassed. I told him one clue is that if he licks an envelope and doesn't taste the glue it is probably this type.

I started to despair. My God, how will he *live*?! But then I reminded myself that I had also licked those envelopes when I first got them. And last week when I set the table for a formal(ish) dinner I yelled upstairs for Jack to Google which side the fork went on. I also thought about the mistakes he will never make. The big ones that have derailed my life at times. Kids like Jack don't like to spend their money. He is not a consumer. He will NEVER go into debt. Can you imagine? He will never feel that shame or fear that 80.1% of Americans feel every day.

Jack's favorite state of being is when he has finished every single thing he has to do for the day and has several hours to just do Jack things, which include watching lots of funny YouTube videos, playing with his "squishies," making books out of pictures he enjoys on the internet or just hopping around humming and laughing at whatever is going on in Jacksonville. The Holy Grail is when all is done, and it is a weekend night. That means he has until three or four in the morning to "do his thing."

Today it is 2018 and he is working on his Eagle Scout Project. Ed is an Eagle Scout and has taken Jack to Scouts every Wednesday night since he was little. Weekend campouts were hard. The weeklong summer camp experience was brutal. Even though Ed always went with him, Jack hated leaving Betsy and me and our comfortable, familiar home. (I loathed summer camp too as a child.) He would dread the week for months in advance and think about it non-stop in the days leading up. It was the unknown, the daddy long legs, missing Betsy and me, unfamiliar food, all of the planned activities. It was so much for him to bear being the way he is. As much as Betsy and I cried when we watched Jack crying in the car as they left, it was good for him to be stretched. These were the times that I was so thankful for Ed. I am a softy for Jack and particularly with Scouts, I am certain that if it weren't for Ed, Jack would not be positioned to be reaching Eagle Scout in the coming year.

I have no background in anything Boy Scout related so this process was a real awakening for me. Think filling out a census (the long form) and having to get signatures by various higher-ups. This can prove tricky, as those suckers can be slippery and quite elusive. We once found ourselves laying in wait at another boy's Eagle Court of Honor ceremony hiding our paperwork under the paper plate of cake so we wouldn't look tacky. Sometimes procuring a signature at a Starbucks rendezvous via text felt like an episode of *The Sopranos*. I found myself giddy as I watched them sign, confused by the involuntary urge to either kiss their feet or give them a lap dance. Getting the final signature from the Jesus figure (the previous had only been John the Baptist) was just the beginning. Next, we sent the PDF document that was approaching twenty pages long to the council to see if they would even approve the project. Jack's was theater-related and involved inventorying all props, organizing them and then storing them in an organized fashion atop newly built shelfs. Ah, there was the rub. You see, the building of the shelves was a different scouts project. The fact that the two projects were going to be connected in this fashion was a new thing. It had never been done before and caused about as much debate and discussion as the first test-tube baby. But after copious hoops, red tape, and traversing attached strings on a unicycle clad in lederhosen, it was accepted. As the days leading up to the first day of the project approach, I could see Jack's anxiety spike. So many details to manage…

So, I worry. I worry about his future. Will he marry, especially if he wants to? Will he live alone, and if so, will he be lonely and think about his childhood - missing it? What will he do for a living? Where will he work? Will he see me die? (I hope). What about Betsy? Will money be an issue and how will he handle that concern? Will he end his life an old man on Medicaid thinking about Betsy, Dad and me and our antics back in the day? If he marries will she be good to him? What things will he endure? Will I be there to help? Then to be fair, and to honor Diane Knollman, I must ask the same questions for Betsy. And where does that get me? Weighted down with dread like watching the *Titanic* slowly leave port. What do I do?

What can I do? I feel desperate at these times.

Then I remember.

I loosen my fists, turn my palms upward and open my hands. I have to give it to Him because the alternative is unbearable. It is now that I wonder how those without a higher power, those without Jesus, make it through. I used to worry about middle school. Would he be able to open his locker, find his way to the different classes, get there on time, pass the classes? Will there be any bullies to break his spirit and heart? Will he secretly have a stomachache before school, not wanting to go? The answers to the first sentences are all yes's, as are the answers to the second. There was a bully, just as I had feared. But Betsy and I drove to his house and confronted him – in front of his parents. Betsy did all the talking because I was too sad and in shock at the situation. It ended well. So yes, I worried about him.

Yet, he made it through. I worried about the high school. Carmel High School has more than five thousand students, but he seems to be faring well. But do I truly want Betsy and Jack to go through life without these trials? Because in them, didn't I myself find my higher power? Betsy chose to eat lunch in a bathroom stall one day because her lunch time had been changed due to a convocation and none of her friends were there. What did she think about in there? Perhaps she prayed. Recalled the truths about her importance in this world and her worth. Not because of who she is but because she is God's daughter. I hope Jack knows this as well. I know we have told him so many times. Yet, for myself, it only becomes true to me in the valleys. I hope we have instilled this strongly enough in the both of them because truly, life is ten percent circumstance and ninety percent attitude.

My son, give me your heart and let your eyes delight in my ways,

Proverbs 23:26

Mari Sandifer

Chapter 20 – Final Thoughts

Many events lead me toward the acceptance of my situation, but one of them stands out because it was so powerful. I was sitting in my car in the parking lot of the supermarket. A precious man named Kenny had just helped load groceries into my trunk. Kenny has some cognitive disabilities and on that particular day he told me how he came to have these challenges.

When he was two years old his family went to pick out a Christmas tree for their home. Kenny wandered away from the family and was struck by a car as he tried to cross the street. The image of this struck me. I wondered how the family had fared after such a tragic accident. "How much therapy would I need after something like that?" I asked myself. "Would I feel responsible? Would I blame Ed? Would Betsy blame herself? And what about the driver?" My brain conjured up the direst of outcomes that could result from such an event. But over the years, Kenny had told me stories about his parents and about visiting his sister and her children in Texas. The joy and hope with which he speaks never indicate any of the collateral damage that I would have expected.

So, I thought, "How many of the tragic circumstances in my head are real? How many are just taking up space and stealing my present joy?" When Jack was told that a fire drill was going to happen at school, it took over our family's life on the days preceding it. The anticipation and fear were so much worse than the actual event. We eventually asked the teacher to stop telling him ahead of time, because in the end it was not giving him any comfort at all to know it was coming. How he envisioned it in his mind was far worse than the reality of it.

When Kenny had finished his story about the accident, I sat in my car and asked myself, "If Jack never converses properly. If he can never live independently. If he never marries or leaves our house. What will that look like?" I came up with a vision. Jack would work at the supermarket too. We lived within biking distance. I would come to know all of the staff and when I would visit, they would say, "Jack! Your mom is here!" He would live with us just as he was now. Our home was more than large enough to provide him with a mini-apartment. It sounded okay to me. Better than okay. I could see myself in that life and it wasn't the worst thing I could imagine. On that day I became okay with the prospect of Jack remaining right where he was and could stop worrying about him "catching up." I put down the heavy load I had been carrying and felt relief and a lightness.

This new vision changed my behavior in a way that not only gave me relief but Jack too. It must have been difficult for him in the early years, sensing that he was disappointing me and never quite getting it right. When I was in elementary school, I loathed recess, because recess meant playing kickball. I was abysmal at sports and it was humiliating to fail publicly every day in front of my friends. But the worst part was the dreaded picking of teams. Not only was I always the last one picked, it got to the point where there would be three of us remaining and one of the team captains would say, "You can just have them." It was horrifying. It was worse than being last. It was being irrelevant.

Can you imagine having to get up every day and go to a job that you weren't good at? Doing something you hated and being forced to fail in front of your peers? Every day? What if you then came home and felt the same pressure from your family? I decided that I wanted Jack to have as much time as possible doing the things he enjoyed. Scouts and Tae Kwon Do have been great opportunities to enlarge his comfort zone, but Jack's brain also requires plenty of down time to explore whatever it is he finds fascinating at the time. Accepting that he would never aspire to join a traveling soccer team was like letting the steam out of a tea kettle.

Now, instead of asking Jack if he wanted to play Frisbee as he got off the bus (he never did) I asked if we should draw buses with a crayon or a sharpie? The sharpie always won out — because they smell delightful. I watched him with fascination as he drew every form of pipe organ pipe in breathtaking detail. No longer did he have to feel he was letting me down when he opted out of doing certain things. We have a huge box in our basement filled with drawings that he made during this time. There were years where everywhere I looked, I saw paper. Paper that had been drawn on, paper that was covered with lists, paper that had been cut into school bus shapes. It was amazing looking through that box as I was writing this book. I wanted to stir up memories from that time. We have so many pictures of him writing, drawing, creating.

Many times, he would carry a list around for days that

he had made, and it would become tattered. We came up with the idea of covering these treasures with clear packing tape. (Think poor man's lamination). But Jack liked when the tape was perfectly smooth, with none of those pesky wrinkles. It worked best to do the taping on an upholstered kitchen chair. I became obsessed with getting it exactly right and I laugh when I recall the times he stood over me watching. I felt like I was in the OR of *Grey's Anatomy*. We eventually bought a real laminating machine, but the box I went through contained many drawings and lists that had been "pack-taped." It made me a bit sad when I wondered what the last thing he ever asked me to tape was. I imagined me going through the process, not knowing it would be the last time. Seeing these reminded me of the times Jack and I were alone together, just the two of us, working on a project or trying to solve a problem. Those were such precious, tender times. It might have appeared indulgent of me to toil over these things, but I knew they were important to him.

In a world fraught with confusion and mixed signals Jack needed an advocate who championed his causes and didn't belittle him for having such specific desires. If I could give him that safe place and honor his wishes, I was glad to do it. In my mind he will always be that earnest little boy who had things in his mind that needed to be transferred to paper and preserved, so that he could hold them, look at them, and allow them to conjure up a magical place. A place that brought him such delight.

Jack creating, 2007.

If you want children to continue dreaming to the moon and beyond, then dream with them, both by sharing your fervent dreams, and by diving heart first into their own.

Vince Gowmon

Chapter 21 - Interview with Jack

During the writing of this book I did a lot of interviewing of Jack, which I taped on my iPhone. I was originally going to incorporate his answers into prose but decided to simply share the questions and answers verbatim so that you could enjoy how he talks as much as I do.

July 28, 2018

M: The humming. You did a lot of humming when you were little. Why?

J: It depended on my mood or what I was thinking of. Usually it meant I was thinking of something exciting or scary. Or something "jumpy"

M: What is a "jumpy" thing?

J: That's when you are REALLY EXCITED about something.

M: Does the type of hum vary or just the thought process behind it?

J: Just the thoughts. The hum is the same.

M: So, the hum sounds the same to us, but it means different things based on what you are imagining. Is that correct?

J: Yes. It's based on feeling or mood.

M: You often paired the humming with an energetic

galloping around the house. What was that?

J: It could be positive or negative. It's just like the humming – but more expressive.

M: What do you remember about preschool?

J: In preschool, one of the things I thought was strange was that some of the kids in my class had autism and they would have random melt-downs. I had no idea why they did that because I couldn't see what was wrong or what they wanted. It didn't seem like they were hurt. I didn't know what was going on. I didn't know if it was stress or not. And it scared me a little bit. Well, a lot actually. I didn't know why they were doing it. I covered my ears and hummed so I didn't have to hear it.

M: Did you ever feel like you had trouble learning things that the other kids learned easily?

J: Yes.

M: What did that feel like?

J: It felt weird. It made me anxious. I felt like I was dumb and silly and stupid. It felt like other kids were getting it, but I wasn't. I never worried that I would get held back. I was afraid the kids would make fun of me if they knew I didn't understand.

M: If you could give me advice for my life, what would that be?

J: From now on, don't do too much. For now, the goal should be to get everything done that you have started. But for the things you don't HAVE to do, just do those things one at a time. One by one. Doing

them all at the same time, it's making your schedule too full. I can see in your room – all of the data, stuff on your white boards, the post its – all that stuff, it scares me. You need to make your schedule more empty. The more you keep trying to do everything at the same time, the more pressure you put on yourself. When you do all of those things together you start to feel like you are going nuts.

M: I can't believe how wise you are. You have given me a lot to think about. Now allow me to change the subject… This book is about you. What do you think about it?

J: I think it's a great way to show parents who have a child on the spectrum how the child might turn out later. Also, what certain things might mean – like the humming and intense interests. I know they are scared because it may seem scary, but it could turn out really well because the child might become interested in very cool things and because they are on the spectrum they will want to learn about these things at a higher level than regular kids might. They can teach themselves.

M: Did kids ever make fun of you at school?

J: Here and there - There have been some bullies, but we have defeated them as they came up against us. Usually I just ignore them because then they get tired of the effort and move on to someone else.

M: I recall that in kindergarten you always wanted to be at the back of the line. What was that?

J: I wanted to be polite and let everyone go ahead. I liked to be at the tail end. I could be the caboose and see everyone in the class ahead of me.

M: Do you want to get married?

J: I don't know yet.

M: What I love about you is how you seem to rise to the occasion. I recall when you were going from Mohawk to Clay Middle School I was scared to death. Because as a rule, middle school can be a brutal place. Tell me what was middle school like for you?

J: Honestly, it wasn't bad. Not as scary as I thought it would be. I was nervous because it was a new school, so I didn't know where anything was. I was used to Mohawk because I had been there, and everyone knew me. The fact that the next three years were going to be at a new school with multiple classrooms and a locker did scare me. But then after I got started it was okay. My sister helped me learn how to open my locker and she walked me to all of my classes in order. We did it like five times until I knew how to do it by myself. I was always afraid I would be late to class and get in trouble. When I would be walking to class, I would imagine different songs in my head based on if I was running late. It was like a soundtrack. Like my life is really a movie. I am super conscientious. I HATE being late and so I am usually early to everything. I just don't want to get in trouble.

M: We LOVE the Carmel school system. You have an IEP, and every year we meet with all of your teachers and the counselor to review your plan and look at your progress. What always struck us through the years was how much they "got" you and sincerely loved you and wanted you to succeed. A new thing, now that you are at the high school, is that you also attend these meetings. What did you think the first time you came to one? Did it feel strange hearing all of us talk about you?

J: I didn't think it was weird at all. It made me feel good that everyone cared, and I felt proud because I am doing well right now. I didn't do well at the very beginning of high school but now I get how to do it better and my grades have improved.

M: How did you feel going from the Middle School to the High School? Carmel High School has almost five thousand students. That's over twice as many as it was when I went there.

J: It wasn't bad at all because they have the Freshman Center, which is like a three-floor triangular prism. It was very easy to find my way around.

M: Next year you will be a sophomore so you will be using the whole school. Does that scare you?

J: Ya. I'm a little nervous about that.

M: I know you like theater and choir. Your sister has a gorgeous voice.

J: And I have a gorgeous voice too.

M: You do. We have talked before about getting into shows and getting choir solos etc. Carmel has so many talented kids. It is quite competitive.

J: I have always wanted to be a soloist. My dream is to sing on stage in front of everyone I know.

M: I think that everyone in the world deserves at least one

standing ovation in their life. Don't you agree?

J: At LEAST one.

M: I think everyone want their "Susan Boyle" moment when they stand up and nobody thinks they can do it. And then they ring the bell and the audience is aghast. And then the audience is on their feet. Glorious.

J: YES! YES! That's what I want to happen to me. I want them to see. But the thing is, I don't know if I can stand just one time. Once I do that, I know I will want it again. I hope that's not pride.

M: I believe you just put words to the plight of every living thespian on earth. I think people just want to feel that they matter. And make a difference.

J: The good thing is that I do get opportunities to do things on stage. So, I am getting closer.

M: You never know.

J: I just need to be patient. God has a plan.

M: Yes, He certainly does. Now I want to switch topics. You go to school and you have kids that you interact with on a daily basis. But you don't do anything socially on the weekends. What does that feel like? Is that your choice? Or do you ever wish you were invited to do things? Do you feel left out or is this actually your preference?

J: I prefer being at home on the weekends because it's very relaxing there. I just like to see you guys and the dogs and just hang out. I do like to go on walks sometimes and I just go by myself, but it's not sad. I like it because it's part of my adventure and in my mind, I am not lonely. And I do enjoy certain YouTube

videos, so I watch those a lot.

M: So, if we were out and about and we saw kids you went to school with as a group doing something, would it make you sad? That you were not invited?

J: No. I would probably just walk over and say "hi" and maybe even talk to them for a few minutes to catch up. But then I would prefer to come back with you or be alone again.

M: So, you do have friends at school?

J: Yes.

M: Do you sit with the same people at lunch?

J: Yea. Sometimes.

M: Have you ever had a situation where you walked into the lunchroom and you couldn't see anyone to sit with? How did that feel? Honestly, that happened to me a few times in high school and I just left and went to my locker and didn't eat that day. It was horrendous.

J: No. I just sit down with people who look nice. I don't care. It's easy.

M: I love that about you. Do they ever say, "That seat is taken?"

J: No. That's just in the movie world. I haven't heard that one yet.

M: That's refreshing. Have you ever felt bullied in certain classes?

J: Ya.

M: What does that look like?

J: Well. It makes me really angry.

M: I would imagine it happens more in larger classes where there might not be structured activity and supervision all the time – like choir and gym?

J: Yes. That is when they might say things to try and get me mad. I tell them to stop but then I just ignore them. I just say, "Do whatever you want. I don't care!" It could be things they say, or they might even push me around. Sometimes I want to punch them. But I know I can tell you and the teacher. It hasn't happened in a long time, but it has happened.

M: I'm so sorry to hear that. Do you recall the first time you thought you might be different than other kids?

J: Yes. It was when I was in actual school, not early childhood. Because some people, they seemed "more normal." But to me they seem tired. Because they were less interested in things. They did not get excited as I did. I got hyped up. They didn't. I like to manifest my excitement by humming and jumping. I did this more when I was younger, but I still do it now. But not at school. Only at home. I DO NOT want to do that at school! Because that's EMBARRASSING! At least for me.

M: When you began to think you were different as a child, did that make you sad?

J: No. Because God made me this way. He loves me.

Life is . . . not about counting the losses and the lost expectations, but rather swimming, with as much grace as can be mustered, in the joy of all of it." – <u>Leisa Hammett</u>

Today is Tuesday, October 1, 2019. I have been working on this book for almost two years. Strangely, I think I will miss it when all is said and done. I recall the night it started. I was with some college friends in Nashville, TN and was pecking away at my computer when my friend Alison's son asked what I was working on. "I'm writing a book," I replied. Boy that sounded strange to say out loud. And pompous. And audacious. I must have been drunk. He was encouraging. "That's so cool!" He said. I had *no idea* what this would entail, but I would do it again in a heartbeat. There are certain things that come up in one's life that you simply "can't not do." This has truly been one of those things.

Betsy is in her second year of college at Ball State University, and Jack is a Junior at Carmel High School. He did finally have his Eagle Scout Board of Review and will

Mari Sandifer

receive his Eagle on November 3, 2019. He is starting to practice driving around the neighborhood but it's hard to imagine him on the highway!

We have had two very exciting developments this year. The Jacksonville Foundation for autism awareness was founded: jacksonvillefoundation.org and a theatre group for kids and young adults who are on the spectrum was launched. It is called The Carmel Spectrum Players: carmelspectrumplayers.org. Our first production is a Night of Cabaret on November 1, 2019 and one of the shows has sold out! I can't wait to see all of those kids performing for family and friends. It will be a magical evening.

"Do not follow where the path may lead. Go instead where there is no path and leave a trail."
Ralph Waldo Emerson

I want to thank you so much for reading this. If it helps one person know that they are not alone, it will have been worth it. God bless you.

Directing the Sunset, 2014.

I praise you because I am fearfully and wonderfully made; your works are wonderful; I know that full well.

Psalm 149:13

About the Author

Mari lives in Carmel, Indiana, with her husband of twenty-six years, Ed, their children Betsy and Jack, and two bichon frises, Charlotte and Dash. She is the founder of the Jacksonville Foundation, which is dedicated to raising autism awareness, and has launched a theatre company called the Carmel Spectrum Players, because every person deserves a platform from which to showcase their talents. Mari grew up in Carmel, IN and attended the Indiana University Kelley School of Business where she earned a BS in marketing and an MBA in finance. She spent 25 years in public accounting, but her CPA license is now inactive (and morbidly obese.) She is the founder of Storycast Network, which specializes in digital storytelling. Her interests include photography, video editing, podcast production, website design, and watching documentaries. Mari is passionate about speaking on the topic of resilience. She is at her best when sharing stories that inspire. If you have such a story, she would love to hear from you and can be contacted through her website at marisandifer.com.

Find your tribe. Love them hard, 2019.

Mari Sandifer